My Adventures in
Zuñi

Frank Hamilton Cushing

Introduction by
Oakah L. Jones, Jr

Also includes An Aboriginal Pilgrimage
and The Father of the Pueblos
by Sylvester Baxter

FILTER PRESS
Post Office Box 95
Palmer Lake, Colorado 80133
(719) 481-2420

Choda	Thirty Pound Rails, 1956
Clemens	Celebrated Jumping Frog, 1965
Matthews	Navajo Weavers and Silversmiths, 1968
Campbell	Wet Plates and Dry Gulches, 1970
Banks	Alferd Packer's Wilderness Cookbook, 1969
Faulk	Simple Methods of Mining Gold, 1969, 1981
Rusho	Powell's Canyon Voyage, 1969
Hinckley	Transcontinental Rails, 1969
Young	The Grand Canyon, 1969
Seig	Tobacco, Peace Pipes and Indians, 1971
Scanland	Life of Pat F. Garrett, 1971
Arpad	Buffalo Bill's Wild West, 1971
Powell	The Hopi Villages, 1972
Schwatka	Among the Apaches, 1974
Powell	An Overland Trip to the Grand Canyon, 1974
Harte	Luck of the Roaring Camp, 1975
Remington	On the Apache Reservations *and* Among the Cheyennes, 1974
Bryan	Navajo Native Dyes, 1978
Underhill	Papago & Pima Indians of Arizona, 1979
Underhill	Pueblo Crafts, 1979
Bennett	Genuine Navajo Rug; How to Tell, 1979
Kennard	Field Mouse Goes to War, 1977
Underhill	People of the Crimson Evening, 1982
Choda	West on Wood, Volume 1, 1986
Duran	Mexican Recipe Shortcuts, 1983
Roosevelt	Frontier Types in Cowboy Land, 1988
Young	Kokopelli, 1990
Garrod	Coyote and the Fish, 1993
Williams	Cripple Creek Conflagrations, 1995
Duran	Kid Kokopelli, 1995
Keen	Blonde Chicana Bride's Mexican Cookbook, 2d ed. 1996
Wilson	Gold Panning in New Mexico, 1996
Bourke & Remington	General Crook in the Indian Country *and* A Scout with the Buffalo Soldiers, 1997
Service	Yukon Poems of Robert W. Service, 1997
Mircos	Gus's Cabin Kitchen, 1997
Hesse	Southwestern Indian Recipe Book, 1997
Penley	Rivers of Wind, 1998
Cushing-Baxter	My Adventures in Zuñi, An Aboriginal Pilgrimage and The Father of the Pueblos

MY ADVENTURES IN ZUÑI

ISBN 0-86541-045-3
Printed in the United States of America

CONTENTS

FRANK H. CUSHING.

INTRODUCTION

Zuñi Pueblo is today one of the most famous Indian pueblos of New Mexico. Located in the extreme western part of the state about thirty miles south of Gallup, it is a village of some three thousand natives known principally for their remarkable skill in the working of turquoise and silver. There is much else, however, that distinguishes Zuñi. It is one of the oldest farming communities in the United States and is also the focal point of an aboriginal ceremonial every December, when the annual Shalako Dance is held. Here at all times one may observe splendidly made pottery and other native crafts.

Yet Zuñi is not the only pueblo of New Mexico and it is not even a unique communal village in the Southwest. It is one of the largest of the nineteen pueblos in New Mexico, ranging in size from Santo Domingo and Zuñi to the relatively few persons comprising Pojoaque Pueblo north of Santa Fe. These far-flung pueblos are the descendants of the highly developed, communally oriented peoples of the Four Corners region. They can be divided linguistically into five major groups: Keres, Tiwa, Tewa, Towa, and Zuñi. Each of the villages has a long and fascinating history, traceable to notable cliff and canyon sites such as those at Aztec, Mesa Verde, Chaco Canyon, Puyé, and Frijoles Canyon. Each has undergone a long-term exposure to European culture, including a Spanish conquest, a lengthy assimilation process resulting from close association with Spanish soldiers, priests, and settlers, and finally more than a century under the control of the United States. All of the pueblos are autonomous with their own systems of government—both secular and religious—and they are located on specified land grants originated by the King of Spain. Farming is their basic way of life, and corn is the principal crop raised in Pueblo country. Although most of the communities are situated along the Rio Grande between Taos and Isleta, a spur of villages runs northwestward from Bernalillo, New Mexico, to Jémez Pueblo, and three pueblos are scattered in the western part of the state—Laguna, Acoma, and Zuñi. When the Spaniards first reached the region in the mid-sixteenth century there were over eighty pueblos, but loss of population, depredations of nomadic enemies such as the Ute, Comanche, Navajo, and various Apache bands, disease, consolidation, and overworking of agricultural lands have caused the reduction to the present nineteen villages.

Perhaps no other single Indian village within the boundaries of the United States today has had such a long, continuous contact with the European as has Zuñi. It was apparently first observed, although not at its present site, by the Franciscan Fray Marcos de Niza in 1539, and Esteban, his Negro servant (and the former companion of Alvar Núñez Cabeza de Vaca). Fray Marcos reported his observations of the "golden cities" from a distance, having obviously seen Hawikuh and perhaps Halona, the ruins of old Zuñi lying south and southwest of the pueblo now located on the banks of the Zuñi River. Francisco Vázquez de Coronado, spurred on by Niza's reports, reached the vicinity of Zuñi the following year and named the site the "Seven Cities of Cíbola." Thereafter the pueblo was visited by Captain Francisco Sánchez Chamuscado in 1580, Antonio de Espejo three years later, and Juan de Oñate after New Mexico was colonized in the final two years of the sixteenth century.

The pueblo had a Franciscan missionary by 1629; in fact, Fray Francisco Letrado was martyred there on February 22, 1632, and the resident missionary was also murdered during the great Pueblo Revolt in 1680. Subsequently, the Zuñis fled to the top of the Taaiyalone Mountain (also known as Thunder or Corn Mountain) east of the present pueblo, but returned to the region to build a new community on the banks of the Zuñi River after the reconquest of New Mexico was completed by Diego de Vargas in the last decade of the seventeenth century. The Zuñis then settled down to a peaceful relationship and established a firm alliance with the Spaniards. They often aided Spanish military expeditions in the following century as auxiliaries, performing numerous services, and in general serving as the Spanish frontier outpost in the West for the remainder of the colonial era. After a short period under Mexican rule, Zuñi was exposed to the visits of many exploratory and cartographic expeditions dispatched by the United States government after New Mexico had been acquired by conquest, occupation, and the Treaty of Guadalupe Hidalgo.

Despite this rich heritage Zuñis's important place in the history of the United States remained obscure for many years to most people of this country. Not until the last quarter of the nineteenth century did it receive the attention it deserved from historians, ethnologists, and archeologists. The present extensive knowledge of the pueblo, its people, their religious beliefs and practices, the political, economic, and social structures, and the general way of life there, all derive from the efforts expended by a few dedicated individuals toward the end of that century.

Frank Hamilton Cushing was indeed a pioneer worker in the field of Zuñi culture. According to Edgar L. Hewett, Cushing was one of the first American ethnologists to realize that the Indians were their own best interpreters and that the study of any Indian culture demanded that one come just as near being a native as possible. Therefore, Cushing went to live with the Zuñis, joining the priesthood, and learning to think as his companions did. Hewett observes that Cushing really translated the "mind of the Zuñi," although he merely got the work started in the intensive study of that pueblo.

Born in Erie County, Pennsylvania, on July 22, 1857, Cushing grew up in Barre Center, New York, where his father was a physician and an assistant surgeon with the Twenty-Eighth New York Volunteers during the Civil War. In "delicate health" from birth (when he had weighed only one and one-half pounds), young Frank did not attend school regularly and he usually did not fit in well with his schoolmates. He developed an early interest in natural history, submitting a scholarly paper to the Smithsonian Institution, which published it in its annual report for 1874.

On the basis of this early publication, as well as Cushing's obvious interest, he was asked by John Wesley Powell to join the staff of the Smithsonian as an assistant in ethnology the following year. Although he possessed no formal training in the field other than a short exposure at Cornell University, Cushing directed the exhibit of the Natural Museum at the Centennial Exposition in Philadelphia during 1876. There he first learned of the Pueblo Indians in far-off territorial New Mexico, and he determined to improve that knowledge at his first opportunity.

As Curator of the Department of Ethnology in the newly created Bureau of American Ethnology, Cushing finally had his chance to select not only a pueblo, but the methods of study he was to employ as a participant on the Smithsonian-sponsored expedition of "Colonel" James Stevenson. He traveled by train with members of that party to Las Vegas, New Mexico. Thereafter the expedition proceeded by mule from Santa Fe to Fort Wingate, a trip of some ten days. Finally, Cushing had his first view of Zuñi and met the natives in late September, 1879. Although he was supposed to stay only three months, Cushing remained at Zuñi under the authorization of the Bureau of Ethnology for the next four and one-half years until he was forced to return to Washington in May, 1884.

Although Edward H. Spicer in his *Cycles of Conquest* states that Cushing was accepted "hospitably" by the Zuñis, and E. DeGolyer (in the introduction to the 1941 Peripatetic Press edition of Cushing's *My Adventures in Zuñi*) states that the natives provided the ethnologist "full cooperation," Cushing's own observations of his early treatment show otherwise. His constant sketching, note-taking, and open challenges of Zuñi taboos reveal that he was regarded with suspicion, considerable distrust, and general hostility bordering on violence during his first few months. Yet his sincerity finally overcame this opposition. Without doubt, one of the fundamental reasons for this change of attitude was his ready adaptation to Zuñi customs, including his willingness to learn the language. He became fluent in Zuñi, studied the village society intensively, and even joined the secret Priesthood of the Bow in 1881 at the invitation of his hosts. Eventually he became one of the Zuñi war chiefs and adopted for his title "First War Chief of Zuñi, U.S. Assistant Ethnologist." It is evident that Cushing concentrated upon the study of creation myths and folktales while living at Zuñi. He was trusted by the Zuñis, who in reality adopted him into their nation and provided him with the name Tenatsali, Medicine Flower, because of the simple remedies he used in the treatment of his adopted uncle at the village.

Cushing, however, was not in residence at Zuñi continuously in the period 1879-1884. In the early summer of 1881 he made an interesting expedition into the Grand Canyon to visit the long-neglected Havasupai nation. En route he visited the Moqui (Hopi) pueblos of eastern Arizona, where he was forced to used his Zuñi language to converse with the Indians there since, as he later reported, Spanish was useless. His account of this journey, originally published in two issues of *The Atlantic Monthly* during 1882, has been reprinted by the Northland Press of Flagstaff, Arizona, under the title of *The Nation of the Willows.* In the foreword of that work Robert C. Euler notes that Cushing's text on the Havasupai "needs little correction or elaboration," a statement which is supported by others who have noted Cushing's meticulous care in preserving accuracy in everything he undertook.

During the following year Cushing returned temporarily to the East, accompanying a group of Zuñi leaders, who had been invited to visit various places in the East to arouse their interest in education and advancement through observation. Sylvester Baxter, a correspondent of the *Boston Herald* and friend of Cushing since Baxter's visit to Zuñi during the summer of 1881, has provided a detailed account of this visit in "An Aboriginal Pilgrimage," published by *The Century Magazine* in 1882.

Apparently this article was an introduction to Cushing's own "My Adventures in Zuñi," which appeared later in the same magazine. The Zuñis traveled by rail in February, 1882, and were received in Washington by President Chester A. Arthur. They then proceeded to Boston and visited Harvard University. At Salem, they openly commended the citizens for their ancestors' persecutions of witches since witchcraft at Zuñi was regarded as a capital crime. Having named Boston the "City of Perpetual Mists," the Zuñis under Cushing's guidance culminated their tour at the Atlantic Ocean, where they scattered prayer sticks and collected water for use in ceremonials back at the pueblo.

While visiting in the East, Cushing had at least two notable personal experiences. Because his hair was eighteen inches long (not then in vogue), he had to have his locks shorn but only after he had consulted with the Zuñi leaders to obtain their acceptance. Also, he married Emily Magill of Washington and brought his bride with him to Zuñi, where the couple resided for the next two years.

Two articles by Boston journalist Sylvester Baxter in the early 1880s (herein reproduced) relate his personal experiences with and observations of Cushing and the Zuñis. One of these, "The Father of the Pueblos" (*Harpers*, 1882, 72-91), is written in flowery language, contains some factual errors, and concentrates upon Zuñi traditions, beliefs, language, folklore, customs, a description of the pueblo, and especially a ceremonial dance. It also provides a personal description of Cushing at Fort Wingate, New Mexico, and an expedition that Sylvester made with Cushing (called "kuishi" by the Zuñis). Sylvester further describes Cushing's room at Zuñi and relates the fact communicated by Cushing that he faced a life-threatening experience from the Zuñis because of Cushing's sketches and portraits of the Zuñis early in his residence at the pueblo. Another article, "An Aboriginal Pilgrimage" (*Century Illustrated Monthly Magazine*, 1882, 526-36) relates the journey of sylvester and Cushing with Zuñi leaders to the eastern United States—Chicago, Washington, D.C., and Massachusetts. The purpose of this trip was to permit the Zuñis to see and take waters from the Atlantic Ocean as specimens that they believed were the "water that brings rain" and that collected near Boston represented for them the easternmost position of the water to the sun. It also gives Zuñi impressions of the train on which they traveled, the cities they visited, and at Salem their opposition to witchcraft. Both articles are important not only for material about Cushing, but for descriptions of Zuñi beliefs and customs.

Perhaps the most important work Cushing carried on in these later years of his residence at Zuñi, in addition to his societal studies, was the preservation of the pueblo's lands from encroachment. To the dissatisfaction of some Indian agents, he aided the Zuñis against the wanderings of Navajo horseherds. Then he turned his attention to assisting them against the encroachments of the invading Anglos. However, this action on his part also led directly to the termination of his activities at Zuñi. Cushing was instrumental in revealing and opposing a land scheme advanced by one Major W.F. Tucker, a plan which would have resulted in the settlement by Anglos of Zuñi lands. Although the young ethnologist, with the help of Baxter's journalistic experience, was successful in countering this scheme, he encountered the wrath of Tucker's father-in-law, General John A. Logan, then Senator from Illinois. Senator Logan advised the director of the Bureau of Ethnology that he would smash the infant agency if Cushing was not recalled. Alleging ill health, Cushing finally departed from Zuñi after many delays, in May 1884.

The young ethnologist's subsequent career is anticlimactic. He continued to work with the Bureau of Ethnology, but his efforts were constantly hampered by poor health, necessitating long absences to recuperate. In these periods of convalescence he occupied himself with translations of Zuñi folktales, completion of his notes, and lecturing as he was able. Although he was named director of the Hemenway Southwestern Expedition to the region of present Tempe, Arizona, in 1886-1887, he had to retire from the field because of illness. On this venture he had been closely associated with famous historians Adolphe F. Bandelier and Frederick Webb Hodge, thus beginning a relationship where many disciplines—including history, ethnology, and archeology—have been considered essential in the study of the development of the Southwest. Cushing was then sent to Florida by the Bureau in the 1890s, and he died there on April 10, 1900, only three months before his forty-third birthday.

Cushing's lengthy residence at Zuñi was the high point of his life, and his many publications emphasizing ceremony, daily life, and social aspects of the Zuñis were his important contributions to scholarship and knowledge of that pueblo. Warren A. Beck in his *New Mexico—A History of Four Centuries* notes that Cushing's accounts of Zuñi creation myths and folktales "remain classics in the treasury of American mythology," even after the passage of three-quarters of a century. Cushing's contributions were not solely in the field of mythology, however. He had considerable influence upon the study of history as well, and his contacts with prominent historians reflect his interdisciplinary impact. He often examined the historical background of the pueblo, concentrating upon the seldom-used area of oral history. In one particular instance Cushing reported that he had been told that the ancestors of the Zuñis had killed one of the "Black Mexicans" (Esteban, the Negro who accompanied Fray Marcos) since they believed there were two types of "Mexicans," the white ones who were good to their people, and the black ones who were like "troublesome beasts." This observation, recorded by Ralph E. Twitchell in his monumental work *The Leading Facts of New Mexican History*, is actually based upon Cushing's own lecture material.

In addition, as Edgar L. Hewett points out in his *Ancient Life in the American Southwest,* Cushing made contributions to archeology and geology. In one instance he shows that the lines on boulders marked the course of ancient irrigation ditches used in diverting streams to cultivated fields. Clark Wissler's *Indians of the United States* indicates that Cushing reported some curious traditions about Zuñi pottery in his article "A Study of Pueblo Pottery as Illustrative of Zuñi Culture Growth," printed in the *Fourth Annual Report of the Bureau of American Ethnology*. Cushing observed that the Zuñi informed him that their forefathers made baskets lined with clay to protect them from burning. Later it was discovered that the dried clay could be lifted out and used in the same way as before. These clay bowls could then be hardened by setting them on the fire. Although scientists scoffed at this idea when it appeared, ethnologists recognize that it is entirely possible that the present Zuñi pottery may have developed in this way.

Most of Cushing's own writings remain buried in little known publications of limited circulation. In fact, in his own time Cushing concentrated on articles in series, lectures, and publications of the Bureau of Ethnology. No major book appeared during his lifetime. His *Zuñi Folk-Tales*, by far the most famous work bearing his name, actually appeared after his death when his wife evidently promoted its publication, although Cushing was responsible for the collection and translation of the tales.

The present edition of "My Adventures in Zuñi" appeared originally as a three-part series in Volumes XXV and XXVI of *The Century Magazine*, 1882-1883. It is easily the best autobiographical account of Cushing's life at Zuñi ever to appear in print. Complete with the original illustrations, this edition is unique in that it is an exact reproduction of the original. In 1941 the Peripatetic Press in Santa Fe did include Cushing's articles as part of a larger work bearing the title *My Adventures in Zuñi*. Although none of the original illustrations were preserved and the format of the publication was altered radically, that edition is useful because of the introductory essay of E. DeGolyer and the inclusion of Baxter's "An Aboriginal Pilgrimage." However, the limited number of copies printed compounded the problem of Cushing's relative obscurity in the mid-twentieth century. Cushing's impact upon the field of ethnology and general scholarship has been a highly controversial issue. DeGolyer noted that the ethnologist was lacking in business ability and was unwilling to delegate authority in the management of affairs during his expeditions. He preferred to work alone and to defy other governmental agencies on occasion. He certainly antagonized the Zuñis repeatedly in his early activities, a defiance which today simply would not be tolerated in any pueblo of New Mexico. In the end, he violated Zuñi trust by publishing many of the secret legends and ceremonial practices of his adopted nation. Oliver LaFarge notes in *The Door in the Wall* that Cushing's publication of Zuñi lore after living with the people of that village was not at all appreciated by the pueblos in general and Zuñi in particular. Furthermore, Cushing evidently contributed greatly to the problem of Zuñi adaptation to the ways of life of the Anglo-Americans. Edward Spicer's *Cycles of Conquest* reveals that this controversy began immediately after the return of the Zuñis from the East in 1882 when one of the elders, Pedro Piño, accepted the new customs and factionalism arose in the pueblo.

On the other hand, one cannot minimize the positive contribution made by Cushing to the public's general knowledge of the Zuñis and to the fields of anthropological and historical scholarship. His residence led to the establishment of many friendly and continuing contacts between the Zuñis and the Anglos. His meticulous research and great care in maintaining accuracy in his publications brought others into these fields, including Bandelier, Hodge, Hewett, and Charles F. Lummis. He was the first to write down legends, societal characteristics, and daily activities of the Zuñis, thus preserving descriptions of events and beliefs, some of which have been lost with the passage of time.

"My Adventures in Zuñi" was republished in hardback by American West Publishing of Palo Alto, California, in 1970. Since the original publication by the Filter Press in 1967, other works have been published about Frank Hamilton Cushing and his residence at Zuñi. These include: Frank H. Cushing, *Zuñi Folk Tales* (Tucson: University of Arizona Press, 1992, reprint of 1901 edition); Jesse Green, ed., *Zuñi Selected Writings of Frank Hamilton Cushing* (Lincoln: University of Nebraska Press, 1979): and Jesse Green, ed., *Cushing at Zuñi: The Correspondence and Journals of Frank Hamilton Cushing,* 1879-1884 (Albuquerque: University of New Mexico Press, 1990). *A Zuñi Artist Looks at Frank Hamilton Cushing* (Zuñi, New Mexico: Pueblo of Zuñi Arts and Crafts, A:Shiwi A:Wan Museum and Heritage Center, 1994), provides forty-three cartoons drawn by Phil Hugte to depict humorous Zuñi views of Cushing and his controversial, disruptive influence at the pueblo.

Frank Hamilton Cushing was indeed a pioneer in the study of Pueblo culture. His work has been widely recognized among scholars not only for its accuracy but also because it was a beginning—one which was a cornerstone in the construction of a vast knowledge of Pueblo culture carried on by historians, ethnologists, archeologists, anthropologists, and sociologists throughout the last two generations. Cushing was The Medicine Flower for the Zuñis, for he supplied the tonic for a languished field of scholarship and revived interest in the Zuñi patient at a critical time when the old ways were in danger of perishing.

OAKAH L. JONES, JR.
Professor Emeritus, Purdue University

PUBLISHER'S NOTE

Oakah L. Jones, Jr., was a major in the United States Air Force and an associate professor of history at the United States Air Force Academy in Colorado when the original edition was published by the Filter Press in 1967. He subsequently served as a professor in the Department of History at the Academy, until 1973. He graduated from the United States Naval Academy at Annapolis, Maryland, where he received his B.S. degree in 1953. After five years of active duty in the Air Force, he entered graduate school at the University of Oklahoma, from which he received his M.A. and later his Ph.D. in history in 1960 and 1964, respectively. He taught for thirteen years at the U.S. Air Force Academy; served a tour in Vietnam; was a lecturer in Latin American history at the University of Colorado, Colorado Springs, for five years; was Chief of Operations and Training at the Inter-American Air Forces Academy in Panama; and after retirement from the Air Force, having served a total of twenty-three years of active military service by 1976, was assistant professor, associate professor, and professor of history at Purdue University, West Lafayette, Indiana, for fifteen years. His fields of interest and specialization are Colonial Latin American History and the Spanish Frontier in Northern Mexico and the United States. He authored five published books: *Pueblo Warriors and Spanish Conquest; Antonio López de Santa Anna; Los Paisanos; Spanish Settlers on the Northern Frontier of New Spain; Nueva Vizcaya; Heartland of the Spanish Frontier;* and *Guatemala in the Spanish Colonial Period.* Also, he edited three other books, published professional articles, and has written over 120 published book reviews in scholarly journals. Now retired from teaching, he lives in Albuquerque, New Mexico, where he continues research and writing, speaking to public and professional audiences, and leading adult study groups to South and Central America.

Frank H. Cushing.

MY ADVENTURES IN ZUÑI.

One hot summer day in 1879, as I was sitting in my office in the ivy-mantled old South Tower of the Smithsonian Institution, a messenger boy tapped at my door, and said:

"Professor Baird wishes to see you, sir."

The professor, picking up his umbrella and papers, came toward the door as I entered.

"Haven't I heard you say you would like to go to New Mexico to study the cliff-houses and Pueblo Indians?"

"Yes, sir."

"Would you still like to go?"

"Yes, sir."

"Very well then, be ready to accompany Colonel Stevenson's collecting party, as ethnologist, within four days. I want you to find out all you can about some typical tribe of Pueblo Indians. Make your own choice of field, and use your own methods; only, get the information. You will probably be gone three months. Write me frequently. I'm in a hurry this evening. Look to Major Powell, of the Bureau of Ethnology, if you want further directions. Good-day."

Thus it happened that, on a sultry afternoon in late September, by no means firmly seated in the first saddle I had ever bestridden, I was belaboring a lazy Government mule just at the entrance of a pass between two great banded red-and-gray sandstone mesas, in the midst of a waterless wilderness. I had ridden from Las Vegas, then the southern terminus of the railway across New Mexico, to Fort Wingate, and over a spur of the Sierra Madres, until here I was far in advance of our little caravan, and nearer the close of my long journey than I had dreamed. Beyond the pass I followed the winding road up a series of cedar-clad sand-hills to where they abruptly terminated in a black lava descent of nearly two hundred feet.

Below and beyond me was suddenly revealed a great red and yellow sand-plain. It merged into long stretches of gray, indistinct hill-lands in the western distance, distorted by mirages and sand-clouds, and overshadowed toward the north by two grand, solitary buttes of rock. From the bases of the latter to a spire-encircled, bare-faced promontory to the right, stretched a succession of cañon-seamed, brown, sandstone mesas, which, with their mantle of piñon and cedar, formed a high, dark boundary for the entire northern side of the basin.

To the left, a mile or two away, crowning numberless red foot-hills, rose a huge rock-mountain, a thousand feet high and at least two miles in length along its flat top, which showed, even in the distance, fanciful chiselings by wind, sand, and weather. Beyond its column-sentineled western end the low sand-basin spread far away to the foot-hills of the gray-and-white southern mesas, which, broken by deep cañons, stretched, cliff after cliff, westward to the hills of the horizon.

Out from the middle of the rock-wall and line of sand-hills on which I stood, through a gate of its own opening, flowed a little rivulet. Emerging from a succession of low mounds beneath me, it wound, like a long whip-lash or the track of an earth-worm, westward through the middle of the sandy plain and out almost to the horizon, where, just midway between the northern buttes and the opposite gray mesas, it was lost in the southern shadows of a terraced hill.

Down behind this hill the sun was sinking, transforming it into a jagged pyramid of silhouette, crowned with a brilliant halo, whence a seeming midnight aurora burst forth through broken clouds, bordering each misty blue island with crimson and gold, then blazing upward in widening lines of light, as if to repeat in the high heavens its earthly splendor.

A banner of smoke, as though fed from a thousand crater-fires, balanced over this seeming volcano, floating off, in many a circle and surge, on the evening breeze. But I did not realize that this hill, so strange and picturesque, was a city of the habitations of men, until I saw, on the topmost terrace, little specks of black and red moving about against the sky. It seemed still a little island of mesas, one upon the other, smaller and smaller, reared from a sea of sand, in mock rivalry of the surrounding grander mesas of Nature's rearing.

Descending, I chanced to meet, over toward the river, an Indian. He was bareheaded, his hair banged even with his eyebrows in front, and done up in a neat knot behind, with long locks hanging down either side. He wore a red shirt and white cotton pantalets, slitted at the sides from the knees down so as to expose his bare legs, and raw-hide soled moccasins. Strings of shell-beads around his neck, and a leather belt around his waist, into which were stuck a boomerang or two, completed his costume. Knitting-work in hand, he left his band of dirty white and black sheep and snuffling goats in charge of a wise-looking, grizzled-faced, bobtailed mongrel cur, and came, with a sort of shuffling dog-trot, toward the road, calling out, "Hai! hai!" and extending his hand with a most good-natured smile.

I shook the proffered hand warmly, and said, "Zuñi?"

"E!" exclaimed the Indian, as he reverentially breathed on my hand and from his own, and then, with a nod of his head and a fling of his chin toward the still distant smoky terraces, made his exclamation more intelligible.

I hastened on with all the speed I could scourge out of my obstinate, kicking mule, down the road to where the rivulet crossed it, and up again, nearer and nearer to the strange structures.

Imagine numberless long, box-shaped, adobe ranches, connected with one another in extended rows and squares, with others, less and less numerous, piled up on them lengthwise and crosswise, in two, three, even six stories, each receding from the one below it like the steps of a broken stair-flight,—as it were, a gigantic pyramidal mud honeycomb with far outstretching base,—and you can gain a fair conception of the architecture of Zuñi.

Everywhere this structure bristled with ladder-poles, chimneys, and rafters. The ladders were heavy and long, with carved slab crosspieces at the tops, and leaned at all angles against the roofs. The chimneys looked more like huge bamboo-joints than anything else I can compare them with, for they were made of bottomless earthen pots, set one upon the other and cemented together with mud, so that they stood up, like many-lobed, oriental spires, from every roof-top. Wonderfully like the holes in an ant-hill seemed the little windows and door-ways which everywhere pierced the walls of this gigantic habitation; and like ant-hills themselves seemed the curious little round-topped ovens which stood here and there along these walls or on the terrace edges.

All round the town could be seen irregular, large and small adobe or dried-mud fences, inclosing gardens in which melon, pumpkin and squash vines, pepper plants and onions were most conspicuous. Forming an almost impregnable belt nearer the village were numerous stock corrals of bare cedar posts and sticks. In some of these, burros, or little gray, white-nosed, black-shouldered donkeys, were kept; while many others, with front legs tied closely together, were nosing about over the refuse heaps. Bob-tailed curs of all sizes, a few swift-footed, worried-looking black hogs, some scrawny chickens, and many eagles—the latter confined in wattled stick cages, diminutive corrals, in the corners and on the house-tops—made up the visible life about the place.

Not an Indian was anywhere to be seen, save on the topmost terraces of this strange city. There hundreds of them were congregated, gazing so intently down into one of the plazas beyond that none of them observed my approach, until I had hastily dismounted, tied my mule to a corral post, climbed the refuse-strewn hill and two or three ladders leading up to the house-tops. The regular

GENERAL VIEW OF ZUÑI.

thud, *thud* of rattles and drum, the cadence of rude music which sounded more like the soughing of a storm wind amid the forests of a mountain than the accompaniment of a dance, urged me forward, until I was suddenly confronted by forty or fifty of the men, who came rushing toward me with excited discussion and gesticulation. One of them approached and spoke something in Spanish, motioning me away; but I did not understand him, so I grasped his hand and breathed on it as I had seen the herder do. Lucky thought! The old man was pleased; smiled, breathed in turn on my hand, and then hastily addressed the others, who, after watching me with approving curiosity, gathered around to shake hands and exchange breaths, until I might have regarded myself as the President, had not an uproar in the court attracted them all away,—all, save one, a young, cadaverous-looking fellow with strange, monkey-like little eyes, who lingered behind and ventured:

"How-li-loo?"

"Pretty well," I replied. "How are you?"

"'At's good," said he, and this useful phrase he employed in every answer to my crowded queries, until I reluctantly concluded that it was the extent of his English. It was amusing to see his efforts, by constantly repeating

FIRST VIEW OF ZUÑI FROM MAL-PAIS MESA.

POOL OF ZUÑI AND WATER-CARRIERS.

this phrase, ducking his head and grinning, to convince the other Indians that he was carrying on a lively conversation with me.

At last, gaining my wished-for position on the edge of the terrace, I came face to face with nearly the whole population of Zuñi. The music had ceased, and the dancers had temporarily retired, but all over the upper terraces were young men in groups and pairs, jauntily mantled in red, green, blue, black, and figured blankets, only the upper portions of their painted faces and occasional patches of their silver-bedecked persons being exposed. Here and there an elaborately plumed straw hat surmounted one of these enveloped statues, aside from which not an article of civilized apparel appeared. Opposite, women and girls, attired in clean, blue-black, embroidered blanket dresses, neat, softly draped head-shawls, and huge-legged, white buckskin moccasins, were standing and sitting on the lower terraces, or in one side of the court below. The older ones were holding their children and talking to them; the younger, intently watching for the dance, or slyly glancing from under their banged hair, which, black as jet and glossy with oil, was combed down over the eyes and parted a little to one side. Old, gray-headed men, muffled in heavy, striped serapes, sat or squatted around, or leaned on their crooked sticks. Innumerable children, some naked, others half clad in tattered cotton shirts and short trousers, were chasing one another about the terraces, wrestling, screeching, or pelting any stray dog that came around, while a few imitated the older people by sitting in silent expectation.

After a brief interval, a priest, with plumed head and trailing white buckskin mantle, gravely stepped in through a tunnel under the houses, scattering on the ground, as he came, sacred meal from a vessel which he held in one hand, while with the other he waved a beautiful wand of macaw plumes. He was followed by some twenty dancers elaborately costumed from head to foot. Close-fitting plumed wigs covered their heads, and black, long-bearded, yellow-eyed masks, with huge rows of teeth from ear to ear, red tongues lolling out between them, gave frightful grinning expressions to their faces. Their half-nude bodies were painted black and yellow, while badges of buckskin were crossed over their shoulders, and skirts of the same material, secured at the waists with elaborately embroidered and fringed sashes, depended to the ankles. Their feet were incased in green and red buskins, and to the legs were bound clanging rattles of tortoise-shell and deer-hoofs. Their necks were decorated with heavy necklaces of shell beads and coral, shining disks of *haliotis* hanging from them in front and behind; while the arms were bedecked with green bands, fluttering turkey plumes, silver bangles and wrist-guards of the same material. Each carried in his right hand a painted gourd rattle, in his left, bow, arrows and long wands of yucca.

As the leader sounded his rattle they all fell into a semicircular line across the plaza, and began stepping rapidly up and down, swaying from side to side, facing first one way, then the other, in perfect unison, and in exact time to their rattles and strange measures of wild music.

Sprawling about the ground in front of and behind the row of dancers, in attitudes grotesque yet graceful, I observed for the first time ten most ludicrous characters, nude save for their skirts and neck-cloths of black tattered blanketing, their heads entirely covered with flexible, round, warty masks. Both masks and persons were smeared over with pink mud, giving them the appearance of reptiles in human form that had ascended from the bottom of some muddy pool and dried so nearly the color of the ground and the surrounding houses that at first it had been difficult to distinguish them.

One of them seated himself a little way off and began pounding with a short, knotty war-club a buffalo-skin bale, which he held between his knees, while the others, motionless save for their heads, which they were continually twisting and screwing about, or nodding in time to the drummer's strokes, kept up a series of comments and banterings which sometimes convulsed the whole throng of spectators with laughter.

In a few moments the leader shook his rattle again, and the dancers ceased as promptly as they had begun, breaking up irregularly and bellowing out long war-cries, brandishing their weapons, and retiring, as they had entered, one by one in the wake of the priest, through the tunnel. Suddenly the motionless, warty-headed figures sprang up, running against one another, crying out in loud tones, and motioning wildly with their long, naked arms. One moment they would all gather around one of their number, as if intensely interested in something he was saying, then as suddenly they would run confusedly about. They would catch up balls and pelt one another most vehemently, such as were struck making great ado about it. One of them discovered me. Immediately he stretched his fingers out and called excitedly to his companions, who pretended to hide behind him and the ladders, peering at me with one or the other of their black, wen-shaped eyes with the most frightened, and, at the same time, ridiculous looks and expression. Their antics were cut short by a renewal of the dance. While one commenced the drumming, another whirled a whizzing stick, and as soon as the others had arranged the costumes of some of the dancers, and had seen them fairly in line, they resumed their sprawling attitudes on the ground.*

Meanwhile, our party had arrived, and the escort had pitched camp in the corral of the mission and school down on the plain about a quarter of a mile north from the pueblo. In one corner, Mr. Hillers, our photographer, and I found a cozy little tent. I spread blankets over the ground, hung pictures and toilet-case on the wind-swayed walls, and thus, with a trunk in either corner, a cot along either side, we made a snug little home for ourselves.

We had not been there long when, to Hillers' disgust and my delight, two or three Indians approached, peered through the fly, and then came in, and squatted on their haunches near the entrance. They took the cigarettes I offered them, and made the interior blue with smoke within a few minutes. They were jolly, talkative fellows, and taught me all sorts of words in their strange, clicky language. Whenever they talked for any length of time, it seemed as if each sentence, long or short, was said in a single breath. At the end of each the speaker would pause, draw a long whiff of smoke from his cigarette, gulp it all into his lungs and begin again, the smoke and words issuing simultaneously from his throat.

Toward sunset, the Gobernador, or head chief, Pa-lo-wah-ti-wa, with some of his *tini-*

PA-LO-WAH-TI-WA, GOVERNOR OF ZUÑI.

* These were the *Ke'ó-ye-mo-shi*, or "Guardians of the 'Sacred Dance,'" whose business is to entertain the spectators during the intervals of the dance, by rude buffoonery and jokes, in which comic speeches and puns play an important part. The office is sacred, and elective annually from among the priesthood of the nation.

A MIDSUMMER TERRACE.

eutes, or sub-chiefs, and the herald of the town, came down to our camp. He was about forty-five years of age, of medium stature, and stooped slightly when walking. He was a grave man of but few words, yet with a kindly expression in his face, which was so finely molded, that in profile it appeared like an Egyptian cameo, the resemblance being heightened by the deep lines of character about his eyes, hollow cheeks, and large, fine mouth, as well as by his rather broad ears shaded with locks of soft jet-black hair. After partaking sparingly of the food we offered him, he thanked us simply and in-

RETURNING FROM THE FIELD.

quired if we wished anything. Learning our desiderata, he gave a few quiet directions to the herald and *tinieutes*, and then departed, not, however, before inviting us to come up on the morrow, to eat peaches and melons with him. Soon after a long musical call proclaimed the governor's orders. From my tent door I could see, on the topmost house of the pueblo, the distant, erect figure of the herald against the twilight sky, a serape thrown gracefully over his shoulders like a Roman toga,—an example of Indian obedience.

Some of us, a young officer and several ladies who had joined our party, strolled up to the pueblo, through a sandy lane and along the winding pathway that led down the hill to a well. As I sat watching the women coming and going to and from the well, "How strangely parallel," I thought, "have been the lines of development in this curious civilization of an American desert, with those of Eastern nations and deserts." Clad in blanket dresses, mantles thrown gracefully over their heads, each with a curiously decorated jar in her hand, they came one after another down the crooked path. A little passageway through the gardens, between two adobe walls to our right, led down rude steps into the well, which, dug deeply in the sands, had been walled up with rocks, like the Pools of Palestine, and roofed over with reeds and dirt. Into this passageway and down to the dark, covered spring they turned, or lingered outside to gossip with new comers while awaiting their chances, meanwhile slyly watching, from under their black hair, the strange visitors from "Wa-sin-to-na." These water-carriers were a picturesque sight, as, with stately step and fine carriage they followed one another up into the evening light, balancing their great shining water-jars on their heads.

We attempted to penetrate a narrow street or two, to enter one of the strange, terrace-bounded courts, but the myriad dogs, with barks and howls in concert, created such a yelping pandemonium that the ladies were frightened, and we returned to camp.

STREET SCENE.

The next morning I climbed to the top of the pueblo. As I passed terrace after terrace the little children scampered for sundry sky-holes, through which long ladder-arms protruded, and disappeared down the black apertures like frightened prairie dogs; while the women, unaccustomed to the sound of shoes on their roofs, as suddenly appeared head and shoulders through the openings, gazed a moment, and then dropped out of sight. Five long flights passed, I stood on the topmost roof.

Spread out below us were the blocks of smoothly plastered, flat-roofed, adobe cells, red and yellow as the miles of plain from which they rose, pierced by many a black sky-hole, and ladder-poles and smoke-bannered chimneys were everywhere to be seen. In abrupt steps they descended toward the west, north, and central plaza, while eastward they were spread out in broad flats, broken here and there by deep courts. The whole mass was threaded through and through by narrow, often crooked, passage ways or streets, more of them lengthwise than crosswise, and some, like tunnels, leading under the houses from court to court or street to street.

The view extended grandly from the outlying, flat lower terraces, miles away to the encircling mesa boundaries north, east, and south, while westward a long, slanting notch in the low hills was invaded to the horizon by the sand-plain through which, like molten silver, the little river ran.

Every school-boy sketches a map of the Zuñi basin when he attempts with uncertain stroke to draw on his slate a cart-wheel. The city itself represents the jagged hub, whence the radiating, wavering trails form the spokes, and the surrounding mesas and hills, the rim. Let some crack across the slate and through the middle of the picture indicate the river, and your map is complete.

In and out, on the diverging trails, the Indians were passing to and from their distant fields, some on foot, some on burro-back, with others of the little beasts loaded from tail to ears with wood, blankets full of melons, pumpkins and corn, or great panniers of peaches. A series of them away out on the bare plain, mere moving specks in the distance, appeared like a caravan crossing a desert waste. Occasionally a half-nude rider, mounted on a swift-footed pony would come dashing in from the hills. Far away he seemed a black object with a long trail of golden dust behind, but his nearer approach revealed remarkable grace of motion and confusion of streaming hair and mane. There was an occasional heavily laden ox-cart, with urchins sprawling over the top, a driver on either side, and leading up the rear a mounted donkey or two; while away to one side, more picturesque than all this, a band of dust-shrouded sheep straggled over the slopes toward their mesa pastures, followed by their solitary herder and his dog.

Strangely out of keeping with the known characteristics of the Indian race were the busy scenes about the smoky pueblo. All over the terraces were women, some busy in the alleys or at the corners below, husking great heaps of many-colored corn, buried to their bushy, black bare heads in the golden husks, while children romped in, out, over and under the flaky piles; others, bringing the grain up the ladders in blankets strapped over their foreheads, spread it out on the terraced roofs to dry. Many, in little groups, were cutting up peaches and placing them on squares of white cloth, or slicing pumpkins into long spiral ropes to be suspended to dry from the protruding rafters.

One of these busy workers stopped, deposited her burden, and hailed a neighboring house-top. Almost immediately an answering echo issued from the red stony walls, and forthwith a pair of bare shoulders seemed to shove a tangled head and expectant countenance up through an unsuspected sky-hole into the sunshine. In one place, with feet over-hanging the roof, a woman was gracefully decorating some newly made jars, and heaps of the rude but exquisite bric-à-brac scattered around her,—while, over in a convenient shadow, sat an old blind man, busy spinning on his knee with a quaint bobbin-shaped spindle-whorl.

Out near the corrals old women were building round-topped heaps of dried sheep dung, and depositing therein with nice care their freshly painted pots and bowls for burning. Others, blankets in hand, were screening their already blazing kilns from the wind, or poking the fires until eddying columns of black pungent smoke half hid them from my view, and made them seem like the "witches and cauldrons" of child-lore.

Children were everywhere, chasing one another over the terraces, up and down ladders, through alleys, and out again into the sunlight. Some, with bows and arrows, sticks and stones, were persecuting in mock chase dogs and hogs alike, as attested by their wild shrieks of delight, or the respondent ceaseless yelps arising seemingly from all quarters of the town at once.

Along the muddy river below the long southern side of the pueblo, more of these youngsters were ducking one another, or playing at various games on the smooth, sandy banks. Women, too, were there engaged in washing wool or blankets on flat stones, or in cleansing great baskets of corn. I was attracted thither and observed that these primitive laundresses had to raise the water with little dams of sand. I smiled as the thought occurred that the first expedition of Americans to Zuñi had been sent here by Government to explore this self-same river, "relative to its navigability."

At the south-western corner of the town, on the river bank, stood the house of the governor. The herald had called a council, and beckoned me to enter. In one of the large rooms the tribal dignitaries were assembling. Some came wrapped closely in their blankets, bearing old canes in their arms,—relics of a forgotten Spanish rule. In a stately, grave manner they approached each of us, shook hands, and took their seats along the northern side of the room. Others, evidently unofficial persons, sauntered inside the door and dropped on their haunches as near to it as possible. Immediately on sitting down, each took out a small piece of plug tobacco, picked it to powder, then, cutting a suitable length of corn-husk with his thumb-nail, rolled a cigarette, and began a protracted smoke. The older ones usually blew the smoke in different directions, closing their eyes, drooping their heads, and muttering a few words which I regarded as invocations.

We told them, as well as we could through our Mexican interpreter, that we were from Washington, whereupon several arose, advanced, and taking our hands breathed from them as though desirous of drinking in the influence of the reverenced name; * that their father was anxious to see how they lived, and to get some of their beautiful articles to show his white children, therefore he had sent us there with many fine things to trade. To everything they replied, "*We-no*" *(Bueno)*. So, securing the large room of the governor's house for Hillers' use, Colonel Stevenson closed the council by giving the multitude a liberal feast of coffee and sugar.

Not many days after the Indians began to bring all sorts of their odd belongings down to the mission. Through the courtesy of Dr. Ealy, the missionary, Colonel Stevenson occupied two of the rear rooms as a trading establishment, and day after day, assisted by his enthusiastic wife, gathered in treasures, ancient and modern, of Indian art and industry. Meanwhile, Hillers and I were busy about the pueblo, the former with photographing, myself with measuring, sketching, and note-taking.

Within a week the Indians could be heard every night singing, and pounding a great drum, in preparation for a dance. It was of a semi-social character, and when, on the morning of the great day, before the assembled multitude, I began sketching in colors the gayly costumed figures below, only lively curiosity was excited and young people gathered so closely around me that it was almost impossible to work. For a long time afterward, as I climbed to the house-tops or sat down in shady old nooks to take notes, the women would gather near, and ask me, with incessant jabber and significant looks, to show them the colored drawings. They were wonder-struck, and would pass their fingers over the figures as though they expected to feel them. Failing in this, they would look at the backs of the leaves, as children look behind mirrors to see what had become of the images.

With a dance that occurred soon after, I was not so successful. It was the sacred water-dance. The long, embroidered cotton garments and strange masks of this wonderful ceremonial would have claimed space in my sketch-books, even had I not been intent on representing everything I saw. When I took my station on a house-top, sketch-books and colors in hand, I was surprised to see frowns and hear explosive, angry expostulations in every direction. As the day wore on this indignation increased, until at last an old, bushy-headed hag approached me, and scowling into my face made a grab at my book and pantomimically tore it to pieces. I was chagrined, but paid no attention to her, forced a good-natured smile, and continued my sketching. Discouraged, yet far from satisfied, the natives made no further demonstrations.

Among my drawings was the portrait of a pretty little girl. An old white-headed grandmother, looking the sketches over one day, recognized this. She shook her head, frowned, and, covering her face with her withered hands, began to cry and howl most dolefully, leaving me abruptly and disappearing into a room adjoining the governor's. At intervals during the remainder of the day, I could hear her talking, scolding, and sobbing over what she regarded as a great misfortune to her family.

I was exercised by this state of feeling, which became, as time went on — especially with those conservators of the ancient régime the world over, old women — more and more virulent. The sketching and note-taking were essential to my work. I was determined not to give them up, but was desirous, so far as possible, of conciliating the Indians. I therefore began with the children. They would scamper up ladders and stand on the roof tops as I passed, but for all that had a lively curiosity concerning me, and would shout to one another, "*Is-ta-shí, Me-lik-í-a!*" — which I rightly divined was, "Just look, the little American is coming!" I began carrying sugar and pretty trinkets in my pockets, and whenever I could tempt some of them near with a lump of the rare delicacy, would pat them on the head and give them the pretty trinkets, or even take the less shy and dirty of them in my arms. I grew in their favor, and within a few days had a crowd of them always at my heels. The parents were delighted, and began to share the affection of their children. Nevertheless, the next time I sketched a dance, all this went for nothing.

Much discouraged, at last I determined to try living with the Indians. Accordingly I moved books, papers, and blankets to the governor's house. On the dirt floor in one corner I spread the blankets, and to the rafters slung a hammock. When the old chief came in that evening and saw that I had made myself at home, he shrugged his shoulders.

"How long will it be before you go back to Washington?" he attempted to ask.

* "Washington" is a term used by nearly all the south-western Indians, not as the name of a place or person, but as that of a government.

"Two months," I signified.

"*Tuh!*" (damn) was his only exclamation as he climbed to the roof and disappeared through the sky-hole.

consisted of a thin adobe wall, about five feet high by as many wide, which stood at right angles with the main wall of the house, and was capped by a structure overhead of thin

POTTERY FIRING.

The room was forty feet in length by twelve in width. The white-washed walls and smooth, well swept floor of plastered mud, paved near the center and at the entrance with slabs of sandstone, gave it a neat appearance. Huge round rafters supported the high, pine-stave ceiling, pierced near one end with a square hole for entrance and exit, and along the center with lesser apertures for the admission of light. Two or three silenite glazed port-holes in the walls served as additional windows, and as many square openings led into other rooms. A carved pine slab, hung on heavy wooden hinges and secured by a knotted string, served as the door of one, while a suspended blanket closed another. A low adobe bench around the room appeared to be the family sitting-place. It was interrupted near one end by the mealing trough and fire-place. The latter sandstone slabs, not unlike the cover of a box, from the corner of which next to the wall rose a flue of long flag-stones to the ceiling. On one side, at its base, a commodious square space was inclosed by narrow stones set edgewise in the ground.

Between the fire-place and the end of the room, eight or ten *metlatls* were slantingly set side by side in a trough of stone,—the mills, coarse and fine, of the household. Along the opposite side of the room was suspended from the rafters a smooth pole, upon which hung blankets, articles of clothing, and various other family belongings. More of the like, including quivers and bows, war-clubs, and boomerangs or "rabbit-sticks," disks of *haliotis* shell, and other ornaments, depended from pegs, and deer or antelope-horns on the walls. Some large, finely decorated water-jars, and a black earthern cooking-pot by the

DECORATING POTTERY.

fire-place, two or three four-pronged stools of wood, sundry blanket rugs and robes, made up the furniture of the apartment. Furnishings and all, it differed not from hundreds of its kind throughout the pueblo, save that conspicuous in one corner was the governor's staff of office,—a silver-knobbed ebony cane, suspended by a faded red ribbon, a present to the tribe, as I afterward learned, from President Lincoln. I did not observe, until I had thrown myself into the hammock, that between the rafters and staves over the center of the room were some beautifully painted and plumed sticks, the guardian gods and goddesses of the household.

As night approached I tried to build a fire and cook supper, but I made but sorry work of it. Unsavory fumes rose from my badly burned bacon, and presently the governor's face appeared at one of the openings in the roof. He regarded operations silently a minute, and then vanished. Soon he followed his feet down the ladder, approached the fire-place, and without a word shoved me aside. Taking my skillet he marched down to the river. When he returned, every trace of the odious bacon had been removed, and replaced by a liberal quantity of mutton and abundant suet. Poking up the fire, the old fellow dexterously cooked the contents brown. Then, placing skillet and all in the center of the floor, he hastened away, soon to return with a tray of curious paper bread in one hand, while in the other, to my surprise, he held a steaming pot of thoroughly boiled coffee.

" Hamon no bueno," he remarked. " Este k'ók-shi, í-tâ," he added; from which amalgamation of Spanish and Zuñi, augmented by suggestive gesticulation, I inferred that he regarded bacon as vile, but Zuñi food prepared in Zuñi fashion as worthy of emphatic recommendation. He did all this after the manner of a man who was performing an unpleasant duty, and when by gesture and incoherent Spanish phrases I expressed my gratitude most extravagantly he merely nodded his head, climbed the ladder, and remarked in Spanish, " Poor fellow," as he disappeared through the sky-hole as before. He probably commiserated me, for I was awakened next morning at the peep of day by the sound of breaking sticks, and turning over in my hammock saw the old fellow busily engaged in preparing a breakfast for me. Nor did he, throughout my long stay among the Zuñis, ever willingly permit me to prepare another meal.

I soon became better acquainted with the domestic life of the Zuñis, and learned where the governor went when he vanished through the sky-hole. His wife's family lived in the second story. There a room much wider than the one below, though not quite so long, accommodated all of them. A large beam through the center gave additional support to the rafters. Against it I struck my head the first time I entered, and, for that matter, nearly every time. I verily believe the Indians, though amused by this, sympathized with me so much that they were kinder than they otherwise would have been. Especially was this the case with the old chief's younger brother,—a constant visitor, himself taller than most of them,—who frequently experienced my difficulty, swearing the explosive oaths of his mother tongue with rare and increasing vehemence with every added experience. Indeed, a bond of sympathy thus arose between us. He soon realized that "Oh!" in American meant "Aí-ii," in Zuñi, and that "Damn" represented "Tuh!" He became morally—or immorally—even more certain, for he occasionally alternated the two expressions, or combined them with more presence of mind than I could have commanded under like circumstances.

The family consisted of the governor's ugly wife, a short-statured, large-mouthed, slant-eyed, bushy-haired hypochondriac, yet the soul of obedience to her husband, and ultimately of kindness to me, for she conceived a violent fancy for me, because I petted her noisy, dirty, and adored little niece. Not so was her old aunt, a fine-looking, straight little old woman of sixty winters, which had bleached her abundant hair as white as snow. She would stand half an hour at a time before me in the middle of the floor, holding the little girl in a blanket on her back, and varying her snatches of lullaby with sighs, meanwhile regarding me with large eyes and half-moon shaped mouth, as though I were a wizard, or a persistent nightmare. The governor did not love her. He called her "Old Ten," which, as he explained after I began to pick up Zuñi and his regards, referred to the number of men she had jilted, and which appellation, when judiciously employed, usually brought hot tears from the old lady's eyes, or unloosed a tongue that the governor avowed "knew how to talk smarting words."

Then there was the governor's brother-in-law, a short, rather thick and greasy man, excessively conceited, ignorant, narrow, and moreover, so ceaselessly talkative, that he merited the name the inventive and sarcastic chief had given him, "Who-talks-himself-dry." I have known him, while dressing in the morning (usually a short process with the Zuñi), to forget, in the ardor of some new scandal, the most important articles of apparel, and issue forth from his couch of skins and robes, very like a half-picked chicken, still talking, and blissfully unaware of his dutifully uncriticised condition.

If the governor loved not "Old Ten," he despised her favorite nephew. This fellow's wife, however, was good-looking, dignified, quiet, modest, and altogether one of the most even-tempered women, red or white, it has been my lot to know. She was always busy with her children, or with the meal-grinding and cookery, occasionally varying these duties with belt-making or weaving. The little niece and her older brother were the only children. The former was a little child, rather too small for her age, bright-eyed, slant-headed like her father, and at once pursy and dirty with abundant food. Though she could not speak plainly, she even thus early gave promise of her father's character, in her ability to make much noise. She was the small "head of the household." All matters, however important, had to be calculated with reference to her. If she slept, the household duties had to be performed on tiptoe, or suspended. If she woke and howled, the mother or aunt would have to hold her, while "Old Ten" procured something bright-colored and waved it frantically before her. If she spoke, the whole family must be silent as the tomb, or else bear the indignation of three women and one man. The governor despised the father too much to join in this family worship. Indeed, while the rest delighted in speaking of this short specimen of humanity by the womanly name of "*Iu-í-si-a-wih-si-wih-ti-tsa,*" the governor called her a "bag of hard howls," and said that she had the habit of storing up breath like a horned toad, which accounted for her extraordinary circumference, and her ability to make a noise in the world.

Little Iú-ní, her brother, was as handsome and as nearly like his mother as boy could be, save that he was rather inconsiderate to dumb things, and to his little sister's hideous dolls.

The aged grandfather of this group was usually absent after wood, or else puttering near the fire-place, or on the sunny terrace, with bits of raw hide, strands of buckskin, or head-scratching. He was lean as Disease, and black as his daughter—which expressed a good deal to her husband, the governor,—with toothless under-jaw and weeping eyes. The Navajos had treated him roughly in his youth, which he showed by the odd mixture of limp, shuffle, and jump in his gait. The

COOKING BREAKFAST.

asthma had tried for years to kill him; but he only coughed and wheezed harder and harder, as winter succeeded winter. So explained his son-in-law, the governor, who, if he ever mentioned him at all, called him "the Ancient Hummer" *(U-mumu-thlä-shi-kia)*— or, to translate into news-boy slang, "Old Buster."

There were two unmarried members of the house; a nephew and an adopted girl. The nephew was an over-grown, heavy-faced, thick-lipped, yellow-haired, blue-eyed blonde, —a specimen of the tribal albinism, a dandy, and the darling of the white-haired "Old Ten." One day, after I had presented the latter with a pane of ruined negative glass, she ventured to compare her favorite with me. My flattering acknowledgments of this compliment made decided winnings of the old woman's hitherto restrained affections. The governor spared this youth no more than the others. With characteristic irony, he called him "The Family Milkman," or "The Night Bird," the latter term referring to his eyes, "which," the governor usually added, "wiggled like those of an owl in strong sunlight." The maiden was jolly, pretty, and coquettish—the belle of "Riverside street." Her lovers were many, but soon, of the long row who waited under the moonlit eaves, only one was admitted— the governor's younger brother, my sympathetic friend. There was but one room in the house in which the two could hope to be left to themselves—mine. Here they came night after night. They paid no attention to the lonely *Mé-lik* in his hammock, but sat opposite in the darkness on the low adobe bench, hour after hour, stroking each other's hands, giggling and cooing in low tones just like so many of my own people of the same age, only in a different language. An occasional smack, followed by feminine indignation, taught me the meaning of "Stop that!" in Zuñi, and the peculiarities of the Pueblo kiss. If the blissful pair remained too late, the slab door would rumble on its wooden hinges, and the governor, preceded by a lighted torch of cedar splints, would stalk in, and, as near as I could make out, rate the young man soundly for his want of respect to the *Wash-intona Me-li-kana*, whereupon the pair would vanish, the maiden giggling and the young man cursing.

I made fair progress in the good graces of this odd group, but still by them, as by the rest of the tribe, I was regarded as a sort of black sheep on account of my sketching and note-taking, and suspicions seemed to increase in proportion to the evident liking they began to have for me. Day after day, night after night, they followed me about the pueblo, or gathered in my room. I soon realized that they were systematically watching me. They were however, pleasant about it, and constantly taught me Mexican and Indian words, so that I soon became able to carry on a conversation with them. My apparent estrangement from the other members of our party aroused in some of them sympathy, in others only additional suspicions. It thus happened that the Indians began to watch me still more strictly, not only by day, but throughout whole nights. No matter how late I lay in the corner of my room, writing, the governor always sat beside me. Not until the last word had been written and I was stretched out in my hammock would he leave. Nor was I even then by myself, for either the governor, or, when he was absent, some one of his relatives or sub-chiefs, slept across the doorway of the room.

Realizing that until I could overcome the suspicion and secure the full confidence of the Indians, it would be impossible to gain any knowledge of importance regarding their inner life, I determined to remain among them until the return of our party from Moqui, whither it was soon to go. It was, therefore with feelings akin to those of a doomed exile that I watched the busy preparations one evening for the departure. This feeling was heightened by the fact that I was by no means intimate with the missionary, and Mr. Graham, the trader, was then temporarily absent from the pueblo. Moreover, I received from most of my party little sympathy in my self-imposed undertaking.

Next morning, when at sunrise I started toward the mission to bid them good-bye, a glance at the distant corral showed that they had all gone; and as I strained my eyes to catch a glimpse of them, the last white-topped wagon of the train disappeared over the far-off lava hills whence I had first caught sight of the Valley of Zuñi.

It had been arranged that my provisions should be left with the missionary. When I applied to him that dreary morning for my coffee, sugar, flour, and other necessaries, he simply replied that he had nothing for me; that the things the Colonel had left were designed for himself. It was with the most gloomy forebodings that I turned toward the pueblo. As I passed along the western end of the town the Indians watched me and commented on my sadness, but several of them assured me that "Zuñi was a good place to live in. So long as one had plenty to eat, why should he feel sad?" I entered my lonely room, and sat down in the hammock, burying my face in my hands. I heard no moccasin footstep, but when I roused up again the old governor was standing before me.

"Why is our little brother sad?" he asked.

"Alas!" I replied, "my friends are all gone, and they have left me nothing."

He looked at me a moment and said, "Little brother, you may be a Washington man, but it seems you are very poor. Now, if you do as we tell you, and will only make up your mind to be a Zuñi, you shall be rich, for you shall have fathers and mothers, brothers and sisters, and the best food in the world. But if you do not do as we tell you, you will be very, very, very poor, indeed."

"Why should I not be a Zuñi?" I replied in despair; and the old man quickly answered, "Why not?"

Leaving me for a few minutes, he soon returned with a steaming bowl of boiled mutton, followed by his kindly old wife, bearing a tray of corn-cakes mixed with *chili* and sliced beef, which, wrapped in husks, had been boiled like meat dumplings.

"There, try that," said the old man, as he placed the bowl in the center of the floor. "Fill your stomach, and your face will brighten."

And the old woman stood admiringly by as I heartily ate my first genuine Zuñi meal.

Although kinder than ever, the governor continued just as faithfully his nightly vigils. One night, after sitting close beside me examining every word I wrote, he threw away his cigarette, and informed me that "it was not well for me to make any more marks on the paper—it was of no use." As I calmly persisted, the next night a grave council was held. It was in the same room, and as I lay in my hammock listening to the proceedings, the discussion grew louder and more and more excited, the subjects evidently being my papers and myself.

When at a late hour the council broke up, the governor approached me, candle in hand, and intently regarded my face for several minutes. He then said:

"The *Keá-k'ok-shi* (Sacred Dance) is coming to-morrow. What think you?"

"I think it will rain."

"And *I* think," said he, as he set his mouth and glared at me with his black eyes, "that you will not see the *Keá-k'ok-shi* when it comes to-morrow."

"*I* think I *shall*," was my reply.

Next morning before I was awake, the herald and two or three *tinieutes* had come in, and, as I arose, were sitting along the side of the house. The old head chief had just prepared my morning meal, and gone out after something. I greeted all pleasantly and sat down to eat. Before I had half finished I heard the rattle and drum of the coming dance. I hastily jumped up, took my leather book-pouch from the antlers, and strapping it

THE DANCE OF THE GREAT KNIFE.

across my shoulder, started for the door. Two of the chiefs rushed ahead of me, caught me by the arms, and quietly remarked that it would be well for me to finish my breakfast. I asked them if the dance was coming. They said they didn't know. I replied that I did, and that I was going out to see it.

"Leave your books and pencils behind, then," said they.

"No, I must carry them wherever I go."

"If you put the shadows of the great dance down on the leaves of your books to-day, we shall cut them to pieces," they threatened.

Suddenly wrenching away from them, I pulled a knife out from the bottom of my pouch, and, bracing up against the wall, brandished it, and said that whatever hand grabbed my arm again would be cut off, that whoever cut my books to pieces would only cut himself to pieces with my knife. It was a doubtful game of bluff, but the chiefs fell back a little, and I darted through the door. Although they followed me throughout the whole day, they did not again offer to molest me, but the people gathered so closely around me that I could scarcely find opportunity for sketching.

As the month of November approached, the cold rains began to fall. Frost destroyed the corn-plants and vines. Ice formed over the river by night to linger a little while in the morning, then be chased away by the midday sun. Not in the least did these forerunners of a severe winter cause the dance ceremonials to abate. The Indians were, to some extent, reassured, when, on the occasion of the next dance, which happened to be a repetition of the first, I did little or no sketching. At another dance, however, I resumed the hated practice, which made matters worse than before. A second council was called. Of this, however, I knew nothing, until afterward told by the old chief. It seems that it was a secret. It discussed various plans for either disposing of me, or compelling me to desist. Among others was the proposal that I be thrown off the great mesa, as were the two "children of the angry waters,"* but it was urged that should this be done, "*Wa-sin-to-na*" might visit my death on the whole nation. In order to avoid this difficulty, others suggested that I be *há-thli-kwïsh-k'ia* (condemned of sorcery) and executed. They claimed that sorcery was such a heinous crime that my execution would be pardoned, if represented to the Americans as the consequence of it. But some of the councilors reminded the others that the Americans had no sorcerers among them, and were ignorant of witchcraft.

At last a plan was hit upon which the simple natives thought would free them from all their perplexities. Surely, no objection could be offered to the "death of a Navajo."† Forthwith the Knife Dance was ordered, as it was thought possible that the appearance of this dance would be sufficient to intimidate me, without recourse to additional violence.

One morning thereafter, the old chief appeared graver and more affectionate toward me than usual. He told me the "*Ho-mah-tchi* was coming,—a very *sa-mu* (ill-natured) dance," and suggested that "it would be well for me not to sketch it." Unaware either of the council or of the functions of the angry dance, I persisted. The old man, a little vexed, exclaimed, "Oh, well, of course, a fool always makes a fool of himself." But he said no more, and I assigned, as the cause of his remarks, superstitious reasons, rather than any solicitude for my safety.

When the great dance appeared, the governor seemed desirous of keeping me at home. During most of the morning I humored him in this. At last, however, fearing I would miss some important ceremonial, I stole out across the house-tops and took a position on one of the terraces of the dance court.

The dancers filed in through the covered way, preceded by a priest, and arranged themselves in a line across the court. Their costumes were not unlike those of the first dance I had witnessed, save that the masks were flatter and smeared with blood, and the beards and hair were long and streaming. In their right hands the performers carried huge, leaf-shaped, blood-stained knives of stone, which, during the movements of the dance, they brandished wildly in the air, in time and accompaniment to their wild song and regular steps, often pointing them toward me.

As the day advanced, spectators began to throng the terraces and court, few, however, approaching to where I was sitting; and the masked clowns made their appearance.

I had been busy with memoranda and had succeeded in sketching three or four of the costumes, when there dashed into the court two remarkable characters. Their bodies, nude save for short breech-clouts, were painted with ashes. Skull-caps, tufted with split corn-husks, and heavy streaks of black under their eyes and over their mouths, gave them a most ghastly and ferocious appearance. Each wore around his neck a short, twisted rope of black fiber, and each was armed with a war-club or ladder-round.

A brief intermission in the dance was the signal for a loud and excited harangue on the part of the two, which, at first greeted with laughter, was soon received with absolute silence, even by the children. Soon they began to point wildly at me with their clubs. Unable as I was to understand all they had been saying, I at first regarded it all as a joke, like those of the *Keó-yi-mo-shi*, until one shouted out to the other, "Kill him! kill him!" and the women and children excitedly rising rushed for the doorways or gathered closer to one another. Instantly, the larger one approached the ladder near the top of which I sat, brandishing his war-club at me. Savagely striking the rounds and poles, he began to ascend. A few Indians had collected behind me, and a host of them stood all around in front. Therefore, I realized that in case of violence, escape would be impossible.

I forced a laugh, quickly drew my hunting-knife from the bottom of the pouch, waved it two or three times in the air so that it flashed in the sunlight, and laid it conspicuously in front of me. Still smiling, I carefully placed my book—open—by the side of the pouch and laid a stone on it to show that I intended to resume the sketching. Then I half rose, clinging to the ladder-pole with one hand, and holding the other in readiness to clutch the knife. The one below suddenly grabbed the skirt of the other and shouted,

* A beautiful bit of folk-lore concerning *Tá-ai-yál-lon-ne*, or Thunder Mountain, and the deluge of the land of Zuñi.

† Figurative expression for any sacrifice of life, either animal or human, at the *Ho-mah-tchi*, or Great Knife Dance and ceremonial,—the ancient war *Ká-ka* of the Zuñis.

"Hold on, he is a *kí-he!* a *kí-he!** We have been mistaken. This is no Navajo." Jumping down to the ground, the one thus addressed glanced up at me for an instant, waved his war-club in the air, breathed from it, and echoed the words of his companion, while the spectators wildly shouted applause. The two held a hurried conference. They swore they must "kill a Navajo," and dashed through the crowd and passage-way out of the court.

The *Keó-yi-mo-shi*, freed from their restraint, rushed about with incessant jabber, and turned their warty eyes constantly in my direction. As I replaced my knife and resumed the sketching, the eyes of nearly the whole assemblage were turned toward me, and the applause, mingled with loud remarks, was redoubled. Some of the old men even came up and patted me on the head, or breathed on my hands and from their own.

Presently a prolonged howl outside the court attracted the attention of all, and the frantic pair rushed in through the covered way, dragging by the tail and hind legs a big, yelping, snapping, shaggy yellow dog. "We have found a Navajo," exclaimed one, as they threw the dog violently against the ground. While he was cringing before them, they began an erratic dance, wildly gesticulating and brandishing their clubs, and interjecting their snatches of song with short speeches. Suddenly, one of them struck the brute across the muzzle with his war-club, and a well-directed blow from the other broke its back. While it was yet gasping and struggling, the smaller one of the two rushed about frantically, yelling, "A knife, a knife." One was thrown down to him. Snatching it up, he grabbed the animal and made a gash in its viscera. The scene which followed was too disgusting for description. It finds parallel only in some of the war ceremonials of the Aztecs, or in the animal sacrifices of the savages of the far North-west. Let it suffice that what remained of the dog at sunset, when the dance ended, was reluctantly given over to its former owner by the hideous pair.†

Whether the Indians had really designed to murder me, or merely to intimidate me, my coolness, as well as my waving of the knife toward the sun, both largely accidental, had made a great impression on them. For never afterward was I molested to any serious extent in attempting to make notes and sketches.

That night, the old chief was profuse in his congratulations and words of praise. I had completed in him, that day, the winning of the truest of friends; and by so doing had decided the fate of my mission among the Zuñi Indians.

* *Kí-he* is an archaic term for "friend." It is now used to signify a spiritual friend, or one who is endowed with sacred powers for the good of mankind, — a spiritual friend to the Kâ-kâ.

† I have since learned that the two, whom I now know very well, belonged to a secret order, members of which are obliged on such occasions to go through this horrible ceremonial.

DANCE PARAPHERNALIA.

KO-LO-WISSI, GOD OF THE PLUMED SERPENT.

MY ADVENTURES IN ZUÑI. II.

WHEN the frost first crackles the corn-leaves in the valley of Zuñi, it is, to the dweller in that desert land, what the first April shower is to husbandmen of New England. For in Zuñi autumn is spring-time. It is the time of soft breezes and hazy beauty of sky, not the days of blazing sun, driving sand-blasts and dust-hidden clouds and distances. You may stand on the topmost terraces of the old pueblo and see the busy harvesters bringing in their last crops, and the old women who have been off among the mountains gathering peaches all day, staggering home at sunset, under huge baskets, strapped across their foreheads, full of the most delicious fruit. As you stroll through the narrow terrace-bounded streets your foot slips on pulpy melon-rinds, and from every dark window-hole dusky faces grin at your mishap. From as many door-ways welcomes greet you in unpronounceable clicks and guttural aspirations, which you are not long in comprehending, for basket after basket of the fruit brought in last evening is set before you. Day after day you may hear from the open plazas the sound of the drum and rattle, telling in strange cadences of the general joy of the time when "the corn grows aged, and the summer birds chase the butterfly to the land of everlasting summer."

THE RETURN OF THE FLOCKS.

It was toward the close of these merry days, one bleak evening in November, just as the red sun had set behind heavy black-bordered clouds at the western end of the plain of Zuñi, and the wind was wildly rushing to the opposite end, with its heavy freightage of sand, dead corn-leaves, and dried grasses, that the herald of Zuñi and I were walking down past the scalp-house toward the buildings of the mission. My companion turned to me with a pleasant smile on his face, and, tucking the corner of his *serape* more closely under one arm, raised his fingers as if to count them.

"Little brother, make your heart glad," said he, "a great festival is now every one's thought. Eighteen days more, and from the west will come the Shá-la-k'o; it welcomes the return of the Kâ-kâ and speeds the departure of the Sun. Make your heart glad, for you shall see it too."

Elated with the change of spirit toward me,

which this indicated on the part of the Indians, who had previously constantly opposed my presence at their ceremonies, I turned to reply, but he was shading his eyes and gazing intently off toward the road over the eastern mesas.

"Look! I wonder who are coming," said he.

A train of wagons was appearing at the crest of the black, distant head-lands. It came but slowly in the dusk, and against the wind-storm, so we returned to the pueblo.

ZUÑI WEAVING.

My room was no longer lonely as at first. Huge blocks of piñon blazed on the hearth, and the Governor, now my inseparable friend, with his watchful, industrious wife, were there to welcome me. Night grew black outside. The wind howled in the chimneys. Rain and hail pelted fiercely down on the roof and against the plates of selenite in the windows. But the fire burned only the more brightly, shooting red tongues of flame up into the black, box-shaped flue, and casting dancing shadows against the white walls and over the stone-paved floor.

Next morning I crossed the pueblo, and looked down over the plain. The storm had ceased. Tents were pitched in the corral of the mission; white-topped wagons stood around, and smoke rose from a little fire in the corner. By these signs I knew that the caravan we had seen was my party returning from Moqui.

Hastening back to tell the good news to my "old brother," as the Governor insisted I should call him now, I met at the entrance

CHIEF PRIEST OF THE BOW.

Colonel Stevenson. Inquiries exchanged, he drew forth and handed me a letter from the Smithsonian Institution, informing me that a continuation of leave had been granted as I requested.

That night, doubtful of the results, I told the Governor that Washington wished me to remain there some months longer, to write all about his children, the Zuñis, and to sketch their dances and dresses.

"Hai!" said the old man. "Why does Washington want to know about our Kâ-kâ? The Zuñis have their religion and the Americans have theirs."

"Do you want Washington to be a friend to the Zuñis? How can you expect a people to like others without knowing something about them? Some fools and bad men have said 'the Zuñis have no religion.' It is because they are always saying such things of some Indians, that we do not understand them. Hence, instead of all being brothers, we fight."

"My little brother speaks wisely, but many of my people are fools, too. He may get in trouble if he pictures the Kâ-kâ too much."

"Suppose I do."

"Well, then, what makes you puff up your face with sad thoughts?" asked the old man impatiently. "Don't you have plenty to eat? When you came here you lived on pig's grease and baked dough, but I threw the light of my favor on you and cooked some mutton. Have you ever had to ask for more? Sister would make all the paper-bread, corn-cakes, and dumplings you could eat, but you will not eat them, and she has grown ashamed. What's the matter anyway?" he persisted. "Do you want to see your mother? Pah? Well you can't, for if Washington says 'You stay here,' what have *you* to say? Now go to bed. You had better cut down that hanging bed of strings, though, and sleep on a couple of sheepskins, like a man. Some night you will dream of 'Short Nose' [my mule], and tumble out of that 'rabbit net,' and then Washington will say I killed you. You just wait till 'Teem-sy' [Colonel Stevenson] and his beasts [the Mexican cook and drivers] go away, I'll make a man of you then;" and with this he leaned back against the adobe bench, with all the complacency of a tolerant, dutiful, and very responsible guardian.

A day or two afterward he approached me with a designing look in his eyes, and snatched off my helmet hat and threw it among some rubbish in the corner, producing from behind his back a red silk handkerchief. Folding this carefully, he tied it around his knee, and then placed it on my head. With a remark denoting disgust, he hastily removed it, and disappeared through a blanket-closed door into a quaint mud-plastered little room. After rummaging about for a time, he came out with a long black silken scarf, fringed at either end, which must have belonged once to some Mexican officer. He wound this round and round my head, and tied the ends in a bow-knot at my temple, meanwhile turning his head from side to side critically. "Good! good!" said the old man. "There, now, go out and show the Zuñis, then travel down to the camp and show the 'Teem-sy-kwe' [Stevenson people] what a sensible man you are, and how much better an *óthl-pan* is than a mouse-head-shaped hat." He also insisted on replacing my "squeaking foot-packs," as he called a pair of English walking shoes, with neat red buckskin moccasins.

Thus, in a blue flannel shirt, corduroy breeches, long canvas leggings, Zuñi moccasins and head-band, heartily ashamed of my mongrel costume, I had to walk across the whole pueblo and down to camp, the old man peering proudly around the corner of an eagle-cage at me as I started. The Zuñis greeted me enthusiastically, but when I reached camp great game was made of me. I returned thoroughly disgusted, determined never to wear the head-band again; but, when I looked for the hat and shoes, they were nowhere to be found. When I asked for them, the Governor said, "No-o-o-o! The Americans are asses. Don't you suppose I know what becomes a man? Here, what have you got that on sidewise for? You Americans *will* stick things on your heads as though your skulls were flat on one side; are they? Well, then! wear your head-band straight and don't make a hat of it. There!" said he, straightening the band. And every morning, just as I was about to go out, he would carefully equip me in the black silk head-band. He took so much satisfaction in this, and it pleased the other Indians so much, that I decided to permit them thenceforth to do with me as they pleased.

One night, toward the close of the month, there appeared in the pueblo the ten Kó-yi-ma-shis. It was for the last time, the Indians told me, for during the old Sun ceremonials others would be elected for the ensuing year. Followed by a great crowd, they went from court to court, repeating in a sing-song, measured tone prayers to the gods and instructions to the people, whom they directed to prepare within four days for the coming festivities. Each of these clowns, save one,—their reputed father,—would start out soberly and properly enough in his recitation, but would soon, as if confused, wander off to some ridiculous, childish nonsense, which would bring down the rebuke of the older one. Forthwith the culprit was hunted forth from the line and replaced by one of his companions. This one, in turn, repeated the failure of the first. Each sally of rude wit was greeted with loud laughter and shouts of applause from the by-standers, who crowded around the little circle and lined the house-tops in the dark. Those near the Kó-yi-ma-shis held torches in order that the grotesque faces might be seen. As soon as the prayer of the oldest one began, however, the torches were lowered, and the whole court was hushed until it was finished. Then the ceremony, varied only in the jokes, was repeated in some other plaza or court.

WOMEN GRINDING CORN.

After all the plazas had been visited, I stealthily followed the retiring Kó-yi-ma-shis to a large room on the south side of the pueblo. A sentinel stood at the door, and no one but these clowns was permitted to enter.

ZUÑI SPINNING.

Nor could I catch more than a glimpse of the fire-lit interior, as the windows were heavily curtained with blankets. I learned that the group had been confined in this room four days and nights, engaged in fasting, prayer, and sacred incantations; so I determined to visit them.

Two days later I collected some tobacco and candles. The evening meal over, I asked where the Kó-yi-ma-shis were.

"They are tabooed," was the reply.

"I know," said I, "but where are they?"

"How do you know? What do you want with them?" the Indians glumly asked.

"They are good men," said I, "and I wish to give them some candles and tobacco."

It happened that an old man whom I knew, was one of the ten. He had temporarily come home after some plumes, and was standing aloof from the rest. A little while after his departure, a messenger came from the high-priest, with the request that I visit them, as "no harm would come from the presence of a *kí-he*." Forthwith, I was instructed how to behave.

"When you go in, little brother, you must breathe on your hand and, as you step into the fire-light, you must say, 'My fathers, how are you these many days?' They will reply, 'Happy, happy'! You must not touch one of them, nor utter a single word in Spanish or American, nor whistle. But you must behave very gravely, for it is *ák-ta-ni* [fearful] in the presence of the gods. If you should happen to forget and say a Spanish word, hold out your left hand and then your right, one foot and then the other, and they will strike them very hard with a wand of yucca."

The messenger guided me to the low door, which I entered, breathing audibly on my hand. Stepping into the brightly lighted center of the room, I started off very well with, "My fathers" *(Hóm a tá-tchu)*, but here broke down, and placing the candles and tobacco on the floor, with a muttered apology, I unfortunately finished, partly in Spanish. Instantly two or three of the sprawling priests started up exclaiming, "*Shu! shu!*" and stretched their hands excitedly toward me. One of them took a wand from the front of the altar, and gravely advanced toward me. Without a word I stretched out my hand, and he hit me a terrific blow directly across the wrist. Never wincing, however, although the pain was excruciating, I stretched out the other hand and my two feet in succession, receiving the hard blows on each. I breathed on my hand and said, *É-lah-kwa* (thanks!). The priest spat on the wand, smiled, and waved it four or five times around my head. The white-haired father of the ten then approached me, placed his finger on his lips as a warning, thanked me for the presents, and asked that the "light of the gods might shine on my path of life." But he directed that I be hustled away, for fear I might commit some other indiscretion.

I had gained my object, however, in merely entering the room. It was large. At the western end stood an altar, composed of tablets of various heights and widths, strangely carved and painted in representation of gods, and set up in the form of a square. At the back were larger tablets, on and through which figures of the sun, moon, and stars were painted and cut. Within the square stood a number of sacred wands of long macaw feathers inserted into beautiful wicker-work handles. Overhead hung the figure of a winged god, a little in front of and below which was suspended horizontally an elaborate cross. It was composed of two tablets, carved to zigzag points at the ends, and joined at the center, so as to resemble a wind-mill with four arms. Numerous eagle-plumes depended from the lower edges of the four arms, on each of which was perched the effigy of a swallow.* Underneath this stood

MAKING HÉ-WÉ (PAPER BREAD).

a large medicine-bowl with terraced edges. It was covered with figures of frogs, tadpoles, and dragon-flies, and contained a clear, yellowish fluid. Over this two of the priests were crouching and muttering incantations. Behind the altar, partly covered with little, embroidered cotton kilts, were the warty masks and the neck-cloths of these priestly clowns. Almost immediately on entering, my guide had uttered prayers and scattered medicine flour over them. All along the walls of the great room, now vivid in the fire-light, now indistinct in the flickering shadows, were painted in red, green, blue and yellow, the figures of animals, birds, human monsters, demons, and significant pictographs.

This little glimpse revealed to me a mysterious life by which I had little dreamed I was surrounded, and I looked forward with curious anxiety to the coming ceremonials.

That night, on my way home, I saw great fires blazing on the south-western hills. I could hear the sound of rattles, and the long, weird cries of the dancers, whose forms were too distant to be seen even against the snow-sprinkled slopes. "The Long-horn and the Hooter, the wand-bearers and the sacred guardians, whom you shall see four days hence," said my brother, as he opened the door to let me in, and motioned with his head in the direction of the sounds.

During the next day, hundreds of Navajos, Moquis, and Indians from the Rio Grande pueblos, gathered in from the surrounding country. Everybody was busy. Oxen were slaughtered by the dozen, sheep by the hundred. In every household some of the men could be seen sewing garments both for themselves and the women. The latter were busily engaged in grinding corn, cooking paper-bread over great polished, black stones, cutting up meat, bringing water, and weaving new blankets and belts. Outside, continual streams of burros, heavily laden with wood, came pouring in from the surrounding mesas.

* I have since learned that this represented the great morning star, and that the swallows were emblematic of the summer rains.

My old brother, however, was none too busy to insist constantly that I should not sketch the "fearful Shá-la-k'o," when they came in from the west. If I would promise this, the party and I should be permitted to see the great ceremonial, which never before had the white man been allowed to look upon.

Toward evening, on the second day following, people began to gather all over the southern terraces, and away out over the plain there appeared seven gigantic, black-headed, white forms, towering high above their crowd of attendants. Gradually they came toward the pueblo, stopping, however, midway in the plain across the river, to perform some curious ceremonials. Meanwhile, eight remarkably costumed figures preceded them, crossed the river, and passed along the western end of the pueblo. These were the same the Governor had told me of. The "Long-horn" and the "Hooter" were clothed in embroidered white garments, and their faces were covered by horrible, ghastly, white masks, with square, black eye and mouth-holes. Their head-dresses were distinguished from each other only by the large white appendages, like bat-ears, attached to one of them, while the other was furnished with a long, green horn, from which depended a fringe of wavy black hair, tufts of which covered the heads of both. They bore in their right hands clattering rattles made from the shoulder-blades of deer, and in their left, painted plumed sticks. Following came two red-bodied, elaborately costumed and ornamented characters wearing round, green helmets, across the tops of which were attached painted round sticks with shell-rattles at either end. They bore in their hands white deer-horns and plumed sticks, and were, with the others, guarded by two nearly nude figures with round-topped, long-snouted, red masks, surrounded at the neck by collars of crow-feathers. They carried rattles like those of the chief figures, and long yucca wands with which to chastise spectators who might approach too near.

THE TOWER OF THE SHADOWS AND THE ROAD OF THE RED DOOR.

All of these were preceded by a gorgeously costumed, bare-headed priest, with streaks of black, shining paint across his eyes and chin, and profusely decorated with turquois ear-rings and shell necklaces. A snow-white deer-skin mantle was thrown gracefully over his shoulders and trailed in the dust behind. He carried a tray of sacred plumes in his hand, and was closely followed by a representation of the fire-god. This was an entirely nude boy, the body painted black and covered all over with many-colored round spots. His face and head were entirely concealed by a round-topped, equally black and speckled mask or helmet. Slung across his shoulder was a pouch made from the skin of a fawn, and in his hand a long, large, smoking torch of cedar bark, which he kept gracefully waving from side to side.

The whole party passed rapidly toward one of the plazas, where a square hole had been dug by the Priest of the Sun. After dancing back and forth four times to the clang of their rattles, uttering at intervals cries of hoo too! hoo too! the four principal characters, with long prayers and ceremonials,* deposited sacrifices of some of the plumed sticks. This ceremonial was repeated in the chief plazas of the pueblo, and outside of it north, south, and east, after which the whole party, just at sunset, retired into one of the immense sacred rooms at the southern side of the town.

After dusk, the giant figures which had been left on the plain across the river came in one by one. They were, by all odds, the most monstrous conceptions I had seen among the Zuñi dances. They were at least twelve feet high. Their gigantic heads were shocks of long black hair with great horns at the sides, green masks with huge, protruding eye-balls, and long, pointed, square-ended, wooden beaks; and their bodies were draped with embroidered and tasseled cotton blankets, underneath which only the tiny, bare, painted feet of the actor could be seen. The spasmodic rolling of the great eyeballs and the sharp snapping of the beak as it rapidly opened and closed, together with a fan-shaped arrangement of eagle-feathers at the back of the head, gave these figures the appearance of angry monster-birds.

To each new house of the pueblo one of these monsters was guided by two priests. The latter were clad in closely fitting buckskin armor and round, helmet-like skull-caps of the same material. Several elaborately costumed flute-players, together with a Kó-yi-ma-shi or two, attended. After prayers and ceremonials before the ladders of the houses to be entered, each, with his two attendant priests, mounted with great difficulty, descended through the sky-hole, and was stationed at one end of the room, near the side of an altar, differing only in details from the one already described as belonging to the Kó-yi-ma-shis. Immense fires of sputtering piñon-wood, and rude, bowl-shaped lamps of grease, brilliantly lighted up each one of these closely curtained rooms.

Toward midnight, my brother explained to me that, in each new room and sacred house of Zuñi, the twelve "medicine" orders of the tribe were to meet, and that, as he was a priest of one of them, I could go with him, if I would sit very quiet in one corner, and not move, sleep, nor speak during the entire night.

As we entered the closely crowded, spacious room into which the first party of dancers had retired, a space was being cleared lengthwise through the center, from the altar down toward the opposite end. With many a hasty admonition, the Governor placed me in a corner so near the hearth that, for a long time, controlled by his directions, I was nearly suffocated by the heat. Along the northern side of the room were the dancers, their masks now laid aside. Conspicuous among them were the two priests, who were engaged in a long, rhythmical prayer, chant, or ritual, over eight or ten nearly prostrate Indians who squatted on the floor at their feet. As soon as this prayer was ended, great steaming bowls of meat, trays of paper-bread, and baskets of melons were placed in rows along the cleared space. A loud prayer was uttered over them by an old priest, who held in his hands a bow, some arrows, and a war-club, and who wore over one shoulder a strange badge of buckskin ornamented with sea-shells and flint arrow-heads.† He was followed by the Priest of the Sun, from the other end of the room. The little fire-god then passed along the array of victuals, waving his torch over them, with which the feast was pronounced ready.

Many of the dishes were placed before the dancers and priests and a group of singers whose nearly nude bodies were grotesquely painted with streaks and daubs of white. They were gathered, rattles in hand, around an immense earthen kettle-drum at the left side of the altar, opposite the now crouching monster. As soon as the feast was concluded, many of the women bore away on their heads, in huge bowls, such of the food as remained.

The singers then drawing closely around the drum, facing one another, struck up a loud chant, which, accompanied by the drumming and the rattles, filled the whole apartment with a reverberating din, to me almost unendurable. Two by two the dancers would rise, step rapidly and high from one foot to the other, until, covered with perspiration and almost exhausted, they were relieved by others. At the close of each verse in the endless chant, the great figure by the altar would start up from its half-sitting posture, until its head nearly touched the ceiling, and, with a startling series of reports, would clap its

* The purification of the pueblos.

† This, as I afterward learned, was Naí-iu-tchi, the Chief Priest of the Bow, or the high-priest of a powerful sacred order of war, in many ways strangely like the Masonic Order, and of which I have since become a member.

long beak and roll its protruding eyes in time to the music.

When the little fire-god took his place in the center of the room, no one relieved him for more than an hour and a half, and I feared momentarily that he would drop from sheer exhaustion. But I learned later that this was a trial ceremonial, and that it was one of the series of preparations which he had to pass through before becoming a priest, to which rank his birth rendered him eligible.

Just as the morning star was rising, the music ceased, the congregation became silent, and the chief dancer was led to the center of the room, where he was elaborately costumed. Then the Priest of the Sun took him up the ladder to the roof, where, facing the east, he pronounced in measured, solemn tones a long prayer to the waning Sun of the Old Year. Descending, he pronounced before the multitude (signalizing the end of each sentence with a clang of his rattles) a metrical ritual of even greater length. Then the spectators gathered around the altar, and hastily said their prayers, the sound of which reminded me of a recitation in concert in a large schoolroom. The sun rose, and they dispersed to their various homes.

Some time after, the dancers, one by one, still in costume, passed over the river toward the southward; and the monsters, to the sounds of chants, accompanied by rude music on the flutes, were guided across to a flat, snow-covered plain, where, in the presence of the assembled priests of Zuñi,— but no others, — they ran back and forth, one after another, over a great square, planted plumed sticks at either end of it, and, forming a procession, slowly marched away and vanished among the southern hills. Toward evening no fewer than seven curious dance-lines of the Kâ-kâ at one time occupied the principal court. Most of that, as well as of the three succeeding nights, were passed in ceremonials at the sacred houses and estufas. With this the great festival was over. The assembled Indian visitors, laden with food and the products of Zuñi looms, departed for their various tribal homes.

During the evening of the last day, just as I was sitting down with the rest around the family supper-bowl, Colonel and Mrs. Stevenson came in to bid me good-bye.

A NIGHT WITH THE SHÁ-LA-K'O.

And on the following morning, long before daylight, their train passed over the lava-hills, and I was once more alone in Zuñi.

During the day I told the Governor that I would follow my friends before two months were over. With great emphasis and a smile of triumph, he replied, "I *guess not.*"

On the evening of the second day he beckoned me to follow, as he led the way into the mud-plastered little room, whither he had unearthed my head-band. In one corner stood a forge, over which a blanket had been spread. All trappings had been removed, and the floor had been freshly plastered. A little arched fire-place in the corner opposite the forge was aglow with piñon, which lighted even the smoky old rafters and the wattled willow ceiling. Two sheepskins and my few belongings, a jar of water and a wooden poker, were all the furnishings. "There," said he, "now you have a little house, what more do you want? Here, take these two blankets,—they are all you can have. If you get cold, take off all your clothes and sleep next to the sheepskins, and *think* you are warm, as the Zuñi does. You must sleep in the cold and on a hard bed; that will harden your meat. And you must never go to Dust-eye's house [the Mission], or to Black-beard's [the trader's] to eat; for I want to make a Zuñi of you. How can I do that if you eat American food?" With this he left me for the night.

ARRIVAL OF THE SHÁ-LA-K'O.

I suffered immeasurably that night. The cold was intense, and the pain from my hard bed excruciating. Although next morning, with a mental reservation, I told the Governor I had passed a good night, yet I insisted on slinging my hammock lengthwise of the little room. To this the Governor's reply was: "It would not be good for it to hang in a smoky room, so I have packed it away." I resigned myself to my hard fate and harder bed, and suffered throughout long nights of many weeks rather than complain or show any unwillingness to have my "meat hardened."

An old priest, whom I had seen at the head of one of the dances, and whose fine bearing and classic, genial face had impressed me, used to come and chat occasionally of an evening with the Governor, in the other room. Often, as he sat in the fire-light, his profile against the blazing background made me wonder if the ghost of Dante had not displaced the old Indian for a moment, so like the profile of the great poet was the one I looked upon. He had conceived a great affection for me, and his visits became more and more frequent, until at last one day he told me his name was Laí-iu-ah-tsai-lun-kia, but that I must forget his name whenever I spoke to him, and call him "father." Now that I wore the head-band and moccasins of his people, his attentions were redoubled, and he insisted constantly that I should dress entirely in the native costume, and have my ears pierced. That would make a complete Zuñi of me, for had I not eaten Zuñi food long enough to have starved four times, and was not my flesh, therefore, of the soil of Zuñi?'

I strongly opposed his often repeated suggestions, and at last he so rarely made them that I thought he had altogether given up the idea.

One day, however, the Governor's wife came through the door-way with a dark blue bundle of cloth, and a long, embroidered red belt. She threw the latter on the floor, and unrolled the former, which proved to be a strip of diagonal stuff about five feet long

ANCIENT MINES IN THE VALLEY OF THE PINES.

by a yard in width. Through the middle a hole was cut, and to the edges, either side of this hole, were stitched, with brightly colored strips of fabric, a pair of sleeves. With a patronizing smile, the old woman said,—

"Put this on. Your brother will make you a pair of breeches, and then you will be a handsome young man."

Under her instructions I stuck my head through the central hole, pushed my arms down into the little blanket sleeves, and gathered the ends around my waist, closely securing them with the embroidered belt. The sudden appearance of the Governor was the signal for the hasty removal of the garment. He folded it up and put it away under the blanket on the forge. Long before night he had completed a pair of short, thin, black cotton trowsers, and secured a pair of long, knitted blue woolen leggins.

"Take off that blue coat and rag necklace," said he, referring to my blue flannel shirt and a tie of gray silk. "What! *another* coat under that. Take it off."

I removed it.

"There, now! Go over into that corner and put these breeches on. Don't wear anything under them."

Then the coarse woolen blanket shirt was again put on as before, only next to my skin. There were no seams in this remarkable garment, save where the sleeves were attached to the shoulders and from the elbows down to the wrists. The sides, a little below the armpits, and the arms inside down to the elbow, were left entirely exposed. I asked the Governor if I could not wear the under-coat.

"No," said he. "Didn't I say you must have your meat hardened?"

Fortunately, however, a heavy gray serape, striped with blue and black, and fringed with red and blue, was added to this costume. One of the young men gave me a crude copper bracelet, and the old priest presented me with one or two strings of black stone beads for a necklace.

The first time I appeared in the streets in full costume the Zuñis were delighted. Little children gathered around me; old women patronizingly bestowed compliments on me as their "new son, the child of Wa-sin-tona." I found the impression was good, and permitted the old Governor to have his way. In fact, it would have been rather difficult to have done otherwise, for, on returning to my room, I found that every article of civilized clothing had disappeared from it.

During my absence for several days on an expedition to the Valley of the Pines in search of mines which had formerly been worked by the Zuñis, the old Governor and his wife industriously plastered my room, whitewashed the walls and even the rafters, spread blankets over the floor, and furnished it in Indian style more luxuriously than any other room in Zuñi. On the wall at one end, the Governor, in recollection of the pictures in officers' quarters which he had seen, had pasted bright gilt and red prints, which no one knows how many years past had been torn from bales of Mexican *bayeta*. Above, carefully secured by little pegs, was a photograph of Colonel Stevenson, which the latter had given the Governor before leaving, and which the Indians had designed as my companion. On my return I was so cordially greeted that I could no longer doubt the good intentions of the Zuñis toward me.

A BIVOUAC IN THE VALLEY OF THE PINES.

My foster father and many other of the principal men of the tribe, now insisted that my ears be pierced. I steadily refused; but they persisted, until at last it occurred to me that there must be some meaning in their urgency, and I determined to yield to their request. They procured some raw Moqui cotton, which they twisted into rolls about as large as an ordinary lead-pencil. Then they brought a large bowl of clear cold water and placed it before a rug in the eastern part of the room. K'iawu presently came through the door-way, arrayed in her best dress, with a sacred cotton mantle thrown over her shoulders and abundant white shell beads on her neck. I was placed kneeling on the rug, my face toward the east. My old father. then solemnly removing his moccasins, approached me, needle and cotton in hand. He began a little shuffling dance around me, in time to a prayer chant to the sun. At the pauses in the chant he would reach out and grasp gently the lobe of my left ear. Each time he grasped, I braced up to endure the prick, until finally, when I least expected it, he ran the needle through. The chant was repeated. and the other ear grasped and pierced in the same way. As soon as the rolls of cotton had been drawn through, both the old man and K'iawu dipped their hands in the water, prayed over them, and, at the close of the prayer, sprinkled my head, and scattered the water about like rain-drops on the floor, after which they washed my hands and face, and dried them with the cotton mantle.

I could not understand the whole prayer; but it contained beautiful passages, recommending me to the gods as a "Child of the Sun," and a "Son of the Coru people of earth" (the sacred name for the priests of Zuñi). At its close, the old man said—"And thus become thou my son, Té-na-tsa-li," and the old woman followed him with, "This day thou art made my younger brother, Té-na-tsa-li." Various other members of the little group then came forward, repeating the ceremonial and prayer, and closing with one or the other of the above sentences, and the distinct pronunciation of my new name.

When all was over, my father took me to the window, and, looking down with a smile on his face, explained that I was "named after a magical plant which grew on a single mountain in the west, the flowers of which were the most beautiful in the world, and of many colors, and the roots and juices of which were a panacea for all injuries to the flesh of man. That by this name,—which only one man in a generation could bear,—would I be known as long as the sun rose and set, and smiled on the Coru people of earth, as a *Shi wi* (Zuñi)."

MY ADVENTURES IN ZUÑI. III.

"The rattled-tailed serpents
Have gone into council;
For the god of the Ice-caves,
From his home where the white down
Of wind in the north-land
Lies spread out forever,
Breathes over our country
And breaks down the pine-boughs."*

THUS say the grandfathers of Zuñi children when the snow-storms whiten the distant mountains and mesas. Next to autumn, winter is the merriest season of the year; merry to the lazy Indians, because a time of rest, festivity, and ceremonial. There is not much to be done; only the wood to be gathered from the mesas and cañons and brought in on "burro-back," the herds to be looked after, and the snow, when it happens to get piled up on the terraces, to be shoveled with wooden spades into blankets, and carried on the head down ladders to the outer edge of the pueblo, and there banked against the corrals. The days, save when some national observance claims the time, or betting over elaborate games in the plazas runs high, are dreary and monotonous enough; but the firelit evenings lengthen into hours of merry conversation. Old gray-heads sit around the hearths, telling their children of the adventures of men and the gods "when the world was young in the days of the new."

When the new-year of 1880 brought such times as these, I had been four months in Zuñi, and was counted one of the Children of the Sun. As I strolled through the streets or over the house-tops, children stopped pelting dogs with snow-balls, or playing checkers with bits of pottery on flat stones, and shouted my new name, "Te-na-tsa-li! Te-na-tsa-li!" at the tops of their shrill little voices. I was able, too, to share somewhat in the conversations and councils of the older ones; no longer did the cigarette of my "brother," the old governor of the tribe, gleam alone when the blazes on the hearth shrank back into the red embers, leaving only the shadows of the night in my little room. No; a dozen red stars glowed and perished with every whiff of as many eager visitors, or burned in concert at the end of each joke or story, revealing strange features which started forth from the darkness, like the ruddy ghosts of some pre-Columbian decade. "Shake the blazes out of the brands," one of these ghosts would say; and another, with a long cedar stick, would poke the brands, till the flames would dart up the black chimney anew, the cigarette stars would fade into ashes in the sunlight of the piñon, when lo! the ancient ghosts became sprawling, half-nude Indians again.

No sooner had I begun to enjoy these evening diversions of the pueblo home than they were interrupted for several days. I then first learned of the existence of thirteen orders or societies, some of which were actually esoteric, others of a less strict nature, but all most elaborately organized and of definitely graded rank, relative to one another. For the introduction here of a few words relative to these organizations, I beg the pardon of the reader; since their existence is a fact of ethnologic importance, and moreover my statements relative to them have been most acrimoniously criticised and persistently disputed.

Functionally they are divisible into four classes: Those of War, of the Priesthood, of Medicine, and of the Chase; yet the elements of every one of these classes may be traced in each of all the others.

Of the first class (Martial) there is but one society—the "A-pi-thlan-shi-wa-ni," or the "Priests of the Bow," at once the most powerful and the most perfectly organized of all native associations, in some respects resembling the Masonic order, being strictly secret or esoteric; it is possessed of twelve degrees, distinguished by distinctive badges.

Of the second class (Ecclesiastical) there is also but one order—the "Shi-wa-ni-kwe," or society of priests, of the utmost sacred importance, yet less strictly secret than the first.

Of the third class (Medical) are the "Ka-shi-kwe" and "A-tchi-a-kwe," or cactus and knife orders—the martial and civil surgeons of the nation; the "Ne-we-kwe" and "Thle-we-kwe," or the gourmands and stick-swallowers; "Bearers of the Wand," who treat diseases of the digestive system; the "Ka-

* An almost literal translation from a Zuñi folk-lore tale of winter.

ka-thla-na-kwe" and "Ma-ke-thla-na-kwe," or grand ka-ka (dance) and grand fire orders, who treat inflammatory diseases; the "Ma-ke-tsa-na-kwe" and "Pe-sho-tsi-lo-kwe," or the lesser fire and insect orders, who treat burns, ulcers, cancers, and parasitic complaints; the "U-hu-hu-kwe," or "Ahem" (cough) order, who treat colds, etc.; and lastly, the "Tchi-to-la-kwe," or rattlesnake order, who treat the results of poisoning, actual or supposed, resulting from sorcery or venomous wounds.

Of the fourth class (Hunters) there is again but one order — the "San-ia-k'ia-kwe," or "Tus-ki-kwe," blood or coyote order — the hunters of the nation.

To all these a fourteenth organization might be added, were it not too general to be regarded as esoteric, notwithstanding its operations are strictly secret and sacred. I refer to the much quoted, misspelled, and otherwise abused "Ka-ka," "the Dance," which is wonderfully perfect in structure, and may be regarded as the national church, and, like the church with ourselves, is rather a sect than a society.

Perhaps the Priesthood of the Bow is the only truly esoteric of all these bodies, since members of it may be admitted to meetings of all the others, while members of the other societies are strictly excluded from the meetings of this.

Early learning this, I strove for nearly two years to gain membership in it, which would secure at once standing with the tribe and entrance to all sacred meetings, as well as eligibility to the Head Chieftaincies. I succeeded, and the memory of my experiences in this connection are to me the most interesting chapter of my Zuñi life.

These orders were engaged in their annual ceremonials, of which little was told or shown me; but, at the end of four days, I heard one morning a deep whirring noise. Running out, I saw a procession of three priests of the bow, in plumed helmets and closely-fitting cuirasses, both of thick buckskin,— gorgeous and solemn with sacred embroideries and war-paint, begirt with bows, arrows, and war-clubs, and each distinguished by his badge of degree,— coming down one of the narrow streets. The principal priest carried in his arms a wooden idol, ferocious in aspect, yet beautiful with its decorations of shell, turquois, and brilliant paint. It was nearly hidden by symbolic slats and prayer-sticks most elaborately plumed. He was preceded by a guardian with drawn bow and arrows, while another followed, twirling the sounding slat which had attracted alike my attention and that of hundreds of the Indians, who hurriedly flocked to the roofs of the adjacent houses or lined the street, bowing their heads in adoration, and scattering sacred prayer-meal on the god and his attendant priests. Slowly they wound their way down the hill, across the river, and off toward the mountain of Thunder. Soon an identical procession followed and took its way toward the western hills. I watched them long until they disappeared, and a few hours afterward there arose from the top of "Thunder Mountain" a dense column of smoke, simultaneously with another from the more distant western mesa of "U-ha-na-mi," or "Mount of the Beloved."

Then they told me that for four days I must neither touch nor eat flesh or oil of any kind, and for ten days neither throw any refuse from my doors, nor permit a spark to leave my house, for "This was the season of the year when the 'grandmother of men' (fire) was precious."

Since my admission to the Priesthood of the Bow, I have been elected to the office of guardian to these gods; have twice accompanied them to their distant lofty shrines, where, with many prayers, chants, and invocations, they are placed in front of their predecessors of centuries' accumulation. Poetic in name and ascribed nature are these cherished and adored gods of war: one is called "A-hai-iu-ta," and the other "Ma-tsai-le-ma," and they are believed to be single in spirit, yet dual in form, the child or children of the God of the Sun, and to guard from year to year, from sunrise to sunset, the vale and children of those they were first sent to redeem and guide. These children receive without question the messages interpreted by their priests from year to year, which unfailingly shape the destinies of their nation toward the "encircling cities of mankind."

When the fast was over and the nation had gladly thrown aside its yoke of restriction with the plumed sacrifices, which were cast into the river or planted on the sandy plain, the nightly sittings were again resumed in my little home. One night, at the pause of a long story, I heard a priest counting his fingers to fix the date of the ceremonials of initiation to be performed, he said, "by the rattlesnakes and fire-eaters." He lamented greatly the loss of some sacred black paint, with which he wished to decorate afresh the tablets of his altar, and was wondering what he would do about it. Conversation recurred to the stories, and I fell to thinking how I could turn the priest's difficulties to account. At last a plan struck me: I took from my trunk a book illustrated with colored prints and pretended to read it before the dim fire-light. As

I had designed, the curiosity of my companions was excited. Then I told them how the pictures had first been painted, and getting my water-color box, which contained some India ink, proceeded to illustrate what I had said. In describing how the colors were made, I dwelt particularly on the ink, saying that it was "made only by the *Chi-ni-kwe*, who were a Celestial people and lived on the back side of the world." I then painted with it a tablet of wood, and the deep black gloss excited their admiration. When I saw this, I hastened to add that "the *black* pigment was most precious; that they might use the other tints, but I could not part with that for an instant." At their usual late hour the company broke up. The priest, on leaving, looked longingly toward the corner wherein I had placed the box of paints, but said nothing. I awaited further developments most anxiously.

Four or five days later he came to me in company with one or two others. It was quite early in the day. As I had hoped, he asked for a "small piece of the Chi-ni-kwe ink." I refused it, repeating what I had already said. For a time he looked blank, but finally asked if I would not *lend* him some of it. Again I refused, saying "I could not trust it out of my sight." Finally, after much consultation with the others, he asked me if I "liked the Mexicans and other fools." I said "No"; then he begged that I should come to the "Chamber of the Rattlesnakes," and bring with me some of the "Chi-ni-kwe black." I purposely hesitated a long time, but finally said that "may-be" I would.

As soon as the embassy had departed, I made up a package of tobacco, candles, etc., with the black paint and an elaborate Chinese ink-stone. Near noon I took my way to the Chamber. I stepped down the ladder with perfect assurance, and observing that all the members were barefooted, drew my own moccasins off and went up to the front of the altar; at the same time speaking the greeting which had been taught me when I visited the "Ko-yi-ma-shi," I deposited the articles one by one, last of all the paint.

Had a ghost appeared in their midst he would not have caused more surprise than my assurance and seeming familiarity with the forms excited in the members of the order. They occupied one of the largest rooms in the town, along the walls of which were painted figures of the gods, among them a winged human monster with masked face, and a giant corn-plant which reached from floor to ceiling and was grasped on either side by a mythologic being. Toward the western end of the room stood the altar, with attendant priests before, behind, and on either side of it. Above all was suspended a winged figure, like the painting on the wall. Between the altar and the blazing hearth were gathered the members, all of whom, save the women, were nearly nude; but elaborate devices in red, white, and yellow paint, representing serpents, suns, and stars, made them appear dressed in skin-fitting costumes. They were at work grinding and mixing paint, adorning costumes, and cleaving blocks of straight-grained cedar into splints about a yard in length, and nearly as thin as grass straws. Others, again, were tying, with strips of "yucca" leaf, the splints thus prepared into bundles about as large as one's arm.

As soon as I had deposited the presents, I approached and saluted the chief-priest, grasped his hands with both my own, and telling him I would "return at evening for the paint," breathed on them and hastily withdrew. On my way home an Indian who had seen me enter cursed me heartily, and said I would suffer for my imprudence, but I paid no attention to him. He told my old brother, however, and when long after dark I threw my serape over my shoulders, the latter asked where I was going. I said "To see the rattlesnakes." "No!" said the old man. "Yes," said I; "if the priest be willing, why should *you* object?" and amid family imprecations I darted out of the door and hurried along the dark streets to the place of meeting. I climbed the ladder and entered, blinking at the flood of light with which the place was aglow. Several of the members started up and motioned me out with their flat hands; but I only breathed deeply from my own, until I reached the place of the old priest. Knowing that Mexican was forbidden, I pretended not to understand what was said, when the latter advised me, in his own language, to go home: on the contrary, I wrung his hand, and, as I pulled off my moccasins, incoherently expressed my thanks for the privilege of remaining, and immediately seated myself as if for the night. It was a heavy "game of bluff"; but utterly bewildered by it, the old priest said nothing for some moments, until, evidently in despair, he lighted a cigarette, blew smoke into the air, uttered a prayer, and then handed the cigarette to me. I smoked a whiff or two, said a prayer in English, and handed the cigarette to the nearest member. I had the satisfaction of hearing them say, "Let him stay; he is no fool, and what if he be—he is our Ki-he, and the 'Beings' will throw the light of their favor upon him, because he cannot understand and knows no better." So they rolled another cigarette and told me I "must smoke all night, and help to make clouds for their little world"; that I "must occasionally give to the fathers (priests and song-masters) my cigarettes, roll more, and never be idle, nor cease smoking." I had never smoked before. The first cigarette made me desperately sick; the second, sicker; so that, when I rose to present it, I reeled and had to sit down again; with the third, the sickness disappeared, and with the fourth I first came to feel the dreamy pleasures of the smoker.

At midnight, a long succession of cries like the voices of strange night-birds penetrated our smoky den. The musicians began to beat their great drum and sing a weird, noisy song, celebrating the origin of their order. Soon a grand company of dancers filed in, costumed like the members of the Rattlesnake order, save that black streaks of paint encircled their mouths, bordered and heightened by lines and daubs of yellow pigment. After passing through a rapid dance, which was attended by the round-headed "Sa-la-mo-pi-a," they settled down along the opposite side of the room. Only the "Sa-la-mo-pi-a" now remained, dancing wildly up and down before the altar, waving his wand of yucca and willow, with which, on occasion, he soundly thrashed the unfortunate sleepers whom his keen little round eyes failed not to discover.

There was now a sudden pause in the music. The Sa-la-mo-pi-a retired, and only members of the two orders remained. Two lads who were undergoing their novitiate, were brought into the middle of the room. The fires and huge grease lamps were freshly kindled and lighted, until the smoke near the ceiling looked almost like the clouds of sunset. A nude functionary brought great armfuls of the splint bundles, and deposited them in front of the hearth. The music struck up —wilder, more mysterious and deafening than ever. The two boys looked wistfully about; one trembled visibly, while the other, more imbued with the spirit of his race, seemed possessed, after the first movements, with a dogged apathy. Two members of the order approached them from behind, pinioned their arms, and stood holding them. All the other members rose, each procured a bundle of the splints, breathed on it, prayed over it, and all, save the leading priests, sat down again; these set up long, terrific cries, rushed toward the fire, howled at it as if in defiance, and stuffed the ends of the splints into the flames and embers. Soon their torches set the place more aglow than ever. They approached the terrified boys, danced, and joined in the wild song, brandishing their flambeaux, and yelling more and more vociferously. Suddenly, two by two, they stepped into the light, thrust the blazing splints into their mouths and throats, drew them forth still aglow with coals, and put the latter out in the mouths of the boys. The stoic stood unmoved, but the other writhed and turned his head piteously; to no purpose, however, for the stalwart priests held him firmly to the fiery ordeal. Two by two, all the members in order of their rank, even the song-masters, went through this process, until just before day-break there remained only the prayers to be said over the wretched pair to complete their initiation. This completed they were conducted to seats, and all present said their prayers before the altar; meal was thrust into my hand and I was dragged up with the rest. A long silence ensued. Sleepy participants nodded, grimaced, fell against one another, re-straightened up, only to repeat again and again the same experience, before daylight sifted in and sunbeams followed through the holes in the blanket curtains. Finally, a woman's voice called down from the roof. One by one she passed down huge bowls of meat broth, red with chili, guava and Indian delicacies, until four rows extended from the end of the room to the altar. She then came in accompanied by a plumed priest of another order; together they said a prayer of presentation, which the priests present replied to with one of thanksgiving. The "bad influence" of the feast was skimmed off with eagle plumes and "thrown up" the altar by a medicine priest. Then the leader called out, "Eat all!" The weary crowd woke up of one accord, and with boisterous jokes, loud smacking, and gurgling exclamations of satisfaction, soon cleared away a good portion of the liberal feast. A bowl of hot broth and meat was set before the novices. It was red with pepper, powder, or chili. They took a mouthful each, and with tears in their eyes desisted, for their lips were as black with cinders as their tongues were white with blisters, but they were bidden to eat. The more timid one refusing was grasped by the nape of the neck by one priest, while another stuffed the hot smoking food down his throat.

Horrible as are these ordeals, they are less so than those of the Cactus order, where the young candidate is scourged with willow wands and cactus thorns, until his naked body is covered with a net-work of ridges and punctures. Far from blaming my foster-people for these things, I look rather to the spirit of their at first imposed, but afterward voluntary sufferings, that they may place themselves beyond the evil they strive to overcome in others; may strengthen the faith of their patients to the sublime power of their medicines, given, they aver, by the gods themselves for the relief of suffering humanity. So, annually, they and their brother orders give public exhibitions of their various powers—sometimes, as is the case with the slat swallowers (or "Bearers of the Wand"), producing injuries for life, or even suffering death; but, nevertheless unflinchingly, year after year, performing their excruciating rites.

When all was over I followed the little ray of golden sunshine, which shot down through the neat covering of the sky-hole, up the slanting ladder and out into the cold winter morning air. A chill seized me before I had reached my little room. Several Indians who noticed my pallor attributed it to my transgressions. They were not long in communicating their thoughts to my old brother, who lamented having allowed me to go. As days passed I grew little better, and a few colds—the result of my scant costume and almost constantly damp, cold feet—at last prostrated me with pneumonia. When I began to recover, I was for weeks almost confined to my room. A walk across the pueblo would exhaust me. During this long illness and convalescence, I was constantly attended by my old brother and K'ia-wu ("sister"). My hammock was once more brought out and strung, and I was allowed more blankets. An almost constant crowd of visitors assembled during the day in my little room, leaving only with the late hours of night. They kept up a steady conversation, and I determined to improve the time by studies of the language. My old brother was delighted. Hour after hour he would sit by my bedside, drilling me in pronunciation and compelling me to say, over and over, the hard new words which he continually produced and explained for my benefit.

I now began to learn that the language spoken by my foster-people is by no means either meager or crude. It has most of the cases, moods, and tenses of the Greek, and like it possessed the singular, dual-plural, plural, and collective-plural numbers. It abounds in synonyms. For instance, the word *much* or *many* is expressed by no fewer than three words: *Em-ma*, *te-u-tcha*, *ko-ho-ma-sho-ko*. For our verb *to know*, five expressions occur, strikingly delicate in their distinctive shades of meaning. *To know*—intentively or abstractly, self-evident knowledge, *ai-yu-ya-na; to know* through the understanding, acquired knowledge, *iu-he-ta; to know*—how to act, speak, think, do or make anything,—methodic knowledge, *an-i-kwa; to know*—a country, road, river, mountain, or place—geographic knowledge, *te-na-di; to know*—a place, person, animal, or personified object—knowledge of acquaintance, *a-na-pi*. Each of these expressions is again capable of modification by grammatic prefixes, suffixes, or interjections; so that more than fifteen almost distinct terms for the one English verb, *to know*, can be produced. Nor are these refinements of meaning limited to this one example; they extend through the whole range of verbs, adverbs, and adjectives of the language. I was at first overwhelmed; but my old brother so invariably pounced upon a wrong use of any apparent synonym, that I soon overcame the difficulty.

To get used to the proper number, however, was not so easy. A friend's face would smile in at my open door. I would say *Kwa-ta* (Come in). He would thank me and obey instantly. Three or four, old and young, would appear; I would address them in the same way. They would look at one another and then at me, and finally begin a discussion as to which of their number I had meant. My old brother would look up and remark *U-kwa-ta*. They would troop in, and he would rate me soundly before them all for such a blunder. But if it happened that two appeared at the door, and I repeated the plural expression, they would unfailingly look over their shoulders as though they expected some one else to follow. Then the old man would laugh at me, swear a little, and call out "*Atch-kwa-ta*." Imagine my surprise when I thought I had mastered these distinctions to find myself yet again sharply rebuked by my old teacher. Several dancers came to my door-way. I said *U-kwa-ta;* they looked offended. "*An*-samu-kwa-ta," said my old brother; the looks vanished before smiles at my ignorance, and my brother explained that they all belonged to "one class" *(ta-nan-ne)*.

He trained me diligently in another peculiarity of his speech. A man may say for "I want" *ha-anti-shi-ma*, but he must not say *ha-kwa-anti-shi-ma* for "I do not want." He must say *kwa* (not) *ha* (I) *anti-shi-ma* (want) *nam-me*, negative ending. "Good" was *k'ok-shi;* "not good," *kwa-k'ok-sham-me;* and this double negative was a sore perplexity, especially when *Kwa* initiated a long sentence and the negative ending was added to each subject verb or adverb as well as to the close of the whole sentence. After I had gained an insight into case, mood, and tense, endings, prefixes, and interjections, my progress was more rapid. The tenses presented the greatest obstacle. One night I went to bed rather discouraged. I dreamed of having gained a clear conception of the tenses (which probably resulted from my long thinking on the subject), and of speaking at great length many of the roots I already knew, with their *proper* prefixes and endings. Next morning I spoke according to my dream, and found to

ZUÑI CEREMONY.

THUNDER MOUNTAIN.

my surprise that the fogs about the whole subject had cleared; for it proved that nearly all Zuñi verbs are regular, my subsequent studies having revealed only four or five exceptions to this rule. Wonder of wonders—a language of regular verbs!

And now began my most interesting studies—in which, alas, my teacher could not help me—of the etymology of the language.

Advocates of the "Bow-wow" theory of the origin of language may find convincing facts among the Zuñis. Take, for instance, the root *a-ti*. It is primarily an exclamation of mortal fear. As *a'-ti*, it means blood. It is a termination expressing violence, as in *la-pa-a-ti*—to shake violently—from *la-pa*, the sound of a shaken blanket, and *ati*. Ta-pa-*at-i*—to rap or pound, as at a door, from *ta-pa*—to tap—and *a-ti*. *Tsi-a-a-ti*—to cut or tear flesh or soft substance—from *tsi-a*, in imitation of the sound of cutting flesh, and *a-ti*. *Teshl-a-ti*—to fear; from *teshl*—to breathe hard, and *a-ti*. *A'-tu*—dark blood—from *a-ti*, the exclamation, and *u-e*—painful,—since black blood is supposed to cause inflammation. *A'-tu*, again, is a violent expression for "get out"; and *tuh* becomes an exclamation of anger, equivalent to our word damn. In fact, the number of words in which elements and roots occur derived from this one exclamation, *a-ti*, are so numerous as to become tedious to others than specialists. I venture, however, on one or two additional examples of derivation through imitation. *Pi-wi-wi-k'e-a* is the sound of a string or thread drawn over a resisting body or through the damp fingers. From this the word *pi-le*—a string—is derived. *Tsu-nu-nu-k'e-a* is the sound of air escaping from the punctured paunch of a slain animal. From it the word *tsu-le* (paunch) is derived. These two words shortened and combined, *pi-tsu-li-a*, signify a round line, a circle—from string and the shape of a paunch, which is round. Thus almost throughout is this remarkable archaic language of the Zuñis built up, bearing in itself no small portion of the primitive history, especially of the intellectual development of the people by whom it is spoken.

During my illness, I was brought into very close contact with the people. I began to think, from the domestic harmony by which I was surrounded, that I had found the long-sought-for social Utopia. One day, however, the governor had a quarrel with his brother-in-law, and with a few sarcastic and telling epithets gathered up his sheep-skins and blankets, came into my room, slammed the door after him, and did not cross the threshold again for months. The weeping but faithful K'ia-wu followed, and thenceforth they took up quarters with me. More than a year elapsed before I had any more privacy while in Zuñi.

The governor was a rare and singular character. I never tire of speaking or writing of him. He was long-suffering to a degree incredible, but silent, emotionless, and unswerving when he had determined. One of his traits was cleanliness. One sunny afternoon he was pottering about the eagle-cage, picking up some hard-wood sticks, and carrying them to the oven, behind which he was carefully piling them. K'ia-wu was on the roof sifting corn, and chatting with some neighboring women. Presently I heard a whine; looking round I saw a large, fine dog limping along, his knee, left eye, lips, mouth, and whole face covered with the yellow spines of a porcupine.

"Ha! a yellow beard comes, and is unhappy," I cried.

"A yellow mustache," echoed and queried the governor.

Why did you tell him?" called K'ia-wu from the roof, for she had just espied the miserable creature.

But the emotionless governor paid attention to neither dog nor remarks. He had just loaded his arms full of the sticks. K'ia-wu, encouraged, warned him that it was his "own uncle's dog." The governor approached the oven with his load; suddenly choosing from it a suitable club, he edged toward the dog, dropped the others, and with two blows across the muzzle dispatched it. Then catching the still struggling brute by the hind-legs, he dragged it toward the river, remarking: "Yellow beards sometimes make little children crazy, and cause thoughts," with which he threw him over the bank, and bade him "go west to the spirit-land of dogs," where he assured him "it would be well to hunt other game than porcupines." Then, under the full shower of K'ia-wu's reproaches, he anxiously asked, "Is supper ready?"

If any of the numerous aggrieved complained to him, he listened gravely with an expression of sympathetic interest, until the plaint was spent, then replied: "I have heard; indeed!" And if this somewhat unsatisfactory reply provoked further remarks, he usually went about what he had to do, or with his characteristic summary manner sent the malcontent home, or left him to plead to an empty room.

K'ia-wu troubled herself much with her husband's actions. They usually slept along the opposite side of my little room Night after night, hour after hour, I have heard her, in the peculiar sing-song tone of her race and sex, lecture the silent governor. The darkness would grow deeper, the embers on the hearth fade to ashes, but the theme lost neither interest nor voice. It used sorely to provoke me; and in my own language, hopelessly striving to sleep, I would sometimes curse both the persistency of the Zuñi Caudle and the silence of the matrimonial stoic. The voice would change, but not cease. "Ho! the younger brother is thoughtful; to-morrow I will fix his bed better," it would say; and the governor, filling the exclamation with the most perfect understanding of the situation, would ejaculate, "Humph!" but no more. Undisturbed, the current would then flow on until later, by considerable distance of the stars, the tone would die away. A moment of dead silence, then a cough from the governor, followed by the bland inquiry:

"Is that all?"

"What more should I say, talkless?" the old woman would reply, in a most injured and ill-controlled tone.

"Well, then" (with a yawn), "let's go to sleep, old girl (*o' ka-si-ki*), for it is time, and the younger brother is restless." With which he would turn over, cough again, and lapse into silence, hopeless to the tongue-weary woman, as evinced by her long-continued, half-smothered sobs.

I had nearly given up seeing a pair of garters which had been promised me, when one day, all bustle and smiles, the "Little mother" came in bearing them.

They were beautiful and well made,—they endure even yet,—and with matronly pride she laid them before me. I paid her liberally, that the subject of Lai-iu-lut-sa should not be resumed. But it was broached to the governor. That night when we were alone, he came and lay down by my side where I was writing.

"Get a big piece of paper," said he, and knowing him, I obeyed.

"Now write." I seized a pencil.

"'Thou comest?' said he, in his own language.

I wrote it and pronounced it.

"Good," said he; then added:

"'Yes; how are you these many days?'

"'Happy!' 'Sit down,' 'Eat.' (Then a tray of bread will be placed before you, but you must be polite, and eat but little, and soon say:) 'Thanks.'

"'Eat enough. You must have come thinking of something. What have you to say?'

"'I don't know.'

"'Oh! yes, you do; tell me.'

"'I'm thinking of you' (in a whisper).

"'Indeed! You must be mistaken.'

"'No!'

"'Aha! do you love me?'

"'Ay, I love you.'

"'Truly?'

"'Yes!'

"'Possibly; we will see. What think you, father?'

"'As you think, my child' (the father will say)."

"What in the name of the moon does all this mean, brother?" I asked him when he had made me read the questions and answers over two or three times, and said I had pronounced them all right.

"It means what you will say to Lai-iu-lut-sa to-morrow night when you go to see her."

I was perplexed. I knew not what to say, as I feared offending the good old man.

"Look here, brother, I can't go to see her; she would laugh at me because I can't speak good Zuñi yet."

"Now that's all I have to say to you," he replied, angrily. "I've done my best for you; if fools will be fools, not even their brothers can help it. I see you propose to live single and have everybody say: 'There goes a man that no woman will have; not even when his brother helps him. No! Do you suppose I am blind? You are no Zuñi; you want to go back to Washington; but you can't, I tell you. You might as well get married; you *are* a Zuñi—do you hear me? You are a fool, too!"

With this, he left me; nor would he speak to me again for many days, save on the most commonplace affairs of life, and then but briefly.

My old father here came to my relief. He persuaded the vexed governor that perhaps Lai-iu-lut-sa did not suit me, and that my refusal of her was no argument against my love for her people. With a sublime sense of his power of diplomacy, he also sat down to have a talk with me the same evening. "You see, my son, I had nothing to say about Lai-iu-lut-sa; don't like her myself," said he, with a smile. "Now had it been Iu-i-tsaih-ti-e-tsa, I should have said, 'Be it well!'" and he waited for me to ask who she was. I kept a wise silence—my old brother kept a sulky one. "She is the finest being in our nation; and *my own niece*," he added, with emphasis.

"I never saw her," said I.

"Is that all?" he exclaimed, eagerly. "Well! she shall bring you a bundle of candle-wood to-morrow evening," he remarked.

"What shall I pay her for it?" I asked.

"Pay her! Nothing, my son; do you wish her to think you a fool, and cover me with shame?"

Next evening, I went to see Mr. Graham, the trader, and staid late. When I returned, a little bundle of pitch-pine was lying by the door-way, and the old governor, getting up with an oath, left the house. Again the girl brought wood, at a time unexpected to me, yet I happened to be absent; and the matter, with many vexatious remarks on my strange behavior, was for a time given up.

The Zuñi customs connected with courtship are curious. Regularly, a girl expresses a fancy for a young man. Her parents or her relatives inform those of the youth, and the latter is encouraged. If suited, he casually drops into the house of the girl, when much the same conversation as the governor tried to teach me ensues; and "if it be well," the girl becomes his affianced, or *Yi-lu-k'ia-ni-ha* (His to be). Thereafter the young couple may be seen frequently together—the girl combing his hair on the sunny terraces, or, in winter, near the hearth, while he sits and sews on articles of apparel for her. When he has "made his bundle," or gathered a sufficient number of presents together,—invariably including a pair of moccasins made from a whole deer-skin,—he takes it to her, and if they are accepted he is adopted as a son by her father, or, in Zuñi language, "as a ward," *Ta-la-h'i*; and with the beginning of his residence with her commences his married life. With the woman rests the security of the marriage ties; and it must be said, in her high honor, that she rarely abuses the privilege; that is, never sends her husband "to the home of his fathers," unless he richly deserves it. Much is said of the inferior position of women among Indians. With all advanced tribes, as with the Zuñis, the woman not only controls the situation, but her serfdom is customary, self-imposed, and willing absolutely. To her belong, also, all the children; and descent, including inheritance, is on her side.

I did not learn, until late in the season, that the midnight Ka-Kas were held thrice monthly during two of the winter months, in all the estufas, or *ki-wi-tsi-we*, of the pueblo, of which there were six, corresponding in Zuñi mythology to the six regions of the universe,—North, West, South, East, Upper, and Lower. One day, however, there came past my house two costumed and masked "Runners of the Ka-Ka." I followed them into a *ki-wi-tsin*. A group of priests near the smoky, rude, stone altar, were gathered, barefooted and praying. I drew my moccasins off, and joined them. A friend among them told me, as we left, that I had "behaved so wisely I could come with him that night and see the Ka-Kas."

What a wonderful night it was! The blazes of the splinter-lit fire on the stone altar, sometimes licking the very ladder-poles in their flight upward toward the sky-hole,—which served at once as door-way, chimney, and window; the painted tablets in one end, with priests and musicians grouped around; the spectators opposite and along the sides; the thin, upward streams of blue smoke from hundreds of cigarettes; the shrill calls of the rap-

A ZUÑI WAR-PARTY.

idly coming and departing dancers, their wild songs, and the din of the great drum, which fairly jarred the ancient, smoke-blackened rafters; the less distinguishable but terribly thrilling "swirr-r" of the yucca-whips, when brought down on some luckless sleeper's head and shoulders; the odors of the burning sacrifices, the tobacco, and of evergreen. All this was impressed indelibly on my memory,— the more impressive, that I was the first of my race to witness it. Wonderful, too, were the costumes and masks. Scaly monsters, bristling with weapons and terrible of voice and manner, with reptile heads; warrior demons, with grinning teeth, glaring eyes, long horns, mats of grizzly hair and beard; grotesque *Ne-wes;* ludicrous *Ko-yi-mashis;* ridiculous caricatures of all things in earth, and of men's strange conceptions. Such made up the sights of the *ki-wi-tsin* of the midnight Ka-Kas. Prayers near morning, distribution of the medicine-water to each of us, and, in Zuñi language, "like leaves in a sand-storm the people severed."

With February came the season of general abandonment to games, when old men and young children were busy with the chances of the thrown stick, the hidden ball, or the contest of matched strength. Even the non-participants, the women, were intensely excited with these peaceful contests; betting, in common with their at all other times less temperate husbands, the choicest articles of apparel, or the most valued items of possession.

One remarkable feature of the Zuñis had impressed me — the well-regulated life they lead. At one season they are absorbed in harvesting, at another in the sacred obligations; now games lead the day, while previously they have been

A ZUÑI FARM-HOUSE.

of such rare occurrence—even among little children—that I had written in my November notes, "The Zuñis have few if any games of chance"; while, had my observations been confined to February, I would have written "A nation of gamesters."

Like most things else in Zuñi, their games were of a sacred nature. Now that the nation "had straightened the thoughts of the impassably terrible 'A-hai-iu-ta' and Ma-tsai-le-ma, the 'beloved two' smiled and willed that, with the plays wherewith they themselves had whiled away the eons of times ancient, should their children be made happy with one another."

So one morning, the two chief priests of the bow (Pi-thlan-shi-wan-mo-so-na-tchi) climbed to the top of the houses, and just at sunrise called out a "prayer-message" from the mount-enshrined gods. Eight players went into a *ki-wi-tsin* to fast, and four days later issued forth, bearing four large wooden tubes, a ball of stone, and a bundle of thirty-six counting straws. With great ceremony, many prayers and incantations, the tubes were deposited on two mock mountains of sand, either side of the "grand plaza." A crowd began to gather. Larger and noisier it grew, until it became a surging clamorous black mass. Gradually two piles of fabrics,—vessels, silver ornaments, necklaces, embroideries, and symbols representing horses, cattle, and sheep,—grew to large proportions. Women gathered on the roofs around, wildly stretching forth articles for the betting; until one of the presiding priests called out a brief message. The crowd became silent. A booth was raised, under which two of the players retired; and when it was removed, the four tubes were standing on the mound of sand. A song and dance began. One by one, three of the four opposing players were summoned to guess under which tube the ball was hidden. At each guess the cries of the opposing parties became deafening, and their mock struggles approached the violence of mortal combat. The last guesser found the ball; and as he victoriously carried the latter and the tubes across to his own mound, his side scored ten. The process was repeated. The second guesser found the ball; his side scored fifteen, setting the others back five. The counts numbered one hundred; but so complicated were the winnings and losings on both sides, with each guess of either, that hour after hour the game went on and night closed in. Fires were built in the plaza, cigarettes lighted, but still the game continued. Noisier and noisier grew the dancers, more and more insulting and defiant their songs and epithets to the opposing crowd, until they fairly gnashed their teeth at one another, but no blows! Day dawned on the still uncertain contest; nor was it until the sun again touched the western horizon, that the hoarse, still defiant voices died away, and the victorious party bore off their "mountains of gifts from the gods."

Another game of the gods was ordered later, in the same way—*Ti-kwa-we*, or the race of the "kicked stick."

Twelve runners were chosen and for four days duly "trained" in the estufas. On the fourth morning, the same noisy, surging crowd was gathered in the principal plaza, the same opposing mountains of goods were piled up. At noon, the crowd surged over to the level, sandy plain beyond the river. They were soon followed by the nude contestants, in two single-file processions, led and closed in by the training-masters. Each had his hair done up in a knot over his forehead, and a strong belt girded tightly about his waist. Either leader carried a small round stick, one painted at the center, the other at either end, with red. When all was ready, each leader placed his stick across his right foot, and, when word was given, kicked it, amid the deafening shouts of the spectators, a prodigious distance into the air and along the trail. Off dashed the runners vying with each other for possession of the stick, and followed by dozens of the wild crowd on foot and on horseback. The course of their race was shaped not unlike a bangle, with either end bent into the center. That is, starting from the river-bank, it went to the southern foot-hills, followed the edge of the valley entirely around, and back whence it had started, in all a distance of nearly twenty-five miles. During the progress of the distant circling race, spectators, including hundreds of the women, lined the house-tops. In much less than two hours and a half the victorious party returned, kicked their stick triumphantly across the river, ran into the plaza, circled around the goods, breathed on their hands, exclaimed, "Thanks! this day we win," and hurried to their estufa, where with great ceremony they were vomited, rubbed, rolled in blankets, and prayed over. Notwithstanding these precautions, they were so stiff within half an hour they could hardly move; yet no one can witness these tremendous races without admiration for the physical endurance of the Indian.

These two games, varied with others which, equally interesting, would require even more space for description, filled the days and nights thenceforward for many weeks. Although I faithfully studied and practiced many of the more complicated of them that I might the better understand them, I remain, notwithstanding many losings and few winnings, yet unable to perfectly master their intricacies. The game of cane-cards, or the "Sacred Arrows," would grace the most civilized society with a refined source of amusement; yet though I have played it repeatedly, I cannot half record its mythic passes, facetious and archaic proverbs, and almost numberless counts. The successful *shos-li*, or cane-player, is as much respected for his knowledge as he is despised for his abandoned, gambling propensities. Great though their passion for game be, the Zuñis condemn, as unsparingly as do we, great excesses in it.

ZUÑI PLANTING.

With the waning of winter the snows had disappeared, and now terrific winds swept daily down from the western "Sierra Blanco," until the plain was parched, and the stinging blasts of sand flew fairly over the top of Ta-ai-yal-lon-ne. Still the races and games went on, until one morning the Priest of the Sun declared aloud that the sun was returning. "Our father has called and his father answers," said the people to one another. The games ceased as if by magic; and the late profligate might now have been seen, early each morning, with hoe and spade in hand, wending his way out to the fields to prepare them for the planting time.

Each morning, too, just at dawn, the Sun Priest, followed by the Master Priest of the Bow, went along the eastern trail to the ruined city of Ma-tsa-ki, by the river-side, where, awaited at a distance by his companion, he slowly approached a square open tower and seated himself just inside upon a rude, ancient stone chair, and before a pillar sculptured with the face of the sun, the sacred hand, the morning star, and the new moon.

There he awaited with prayer and sacred song the rising of the sun. Not many such pilgrimages are made ere the "Suns look at each other," and the shadows of the solar monolith, the monument of Thunder Mountain, and the pillar of the gardens of Zuñi, "lie along the same trail." Then the priest blesses, thanks, and exhorts his father, while the warrior guardian responds as he cuts the last notch in his pine-wood calendar, and both hasten back to call from the house-tops the glad tidings of the return of spring. Nor may the Sun Priest err in his watch of Time's flight; for many are the houses in Zuñi with scores on their walls or ancient plates imbedded therein, while opposite, a convenient window or small port-hole lets in the light of the rising sun, which shines but two mornings in the three hundred and sixty-five on the same place. Wonderfully reliable and ingenious are these rude systems of orientation, by which the religion, the labors, and even the pastimes of the Zuñis are regulated.

Each day whole families hastened away to their planting pueblos, or distant farm-houses, but the sand-storms abated not. At night there was not a zephyr, but soon after sunrise, away off over the western rim of the plain, a golden, writhing wave of dust could be seen, followed by another and another, and rising higher and higher, until as it swirled over the pueblo it fairly darkened the sky, increasing in column and height until the sun went down; then retreating after him and covering the plain, not with golden, but with blood-red waves, matching in brilliancy and shifting beauty the blazing clouds of the evening skies.

I well remember the morning my old brother and I parted for the first time. He lingered by me long after the others had gone and his burros had strayed far up the valley trail. Finally, he took me gently by the hand, saying:

"Ah! little brother, my heart is like the clods I go to break—heavy! For I have grown to you as one stalk grows to another when they are planted together. Poor little brother, may the light of their favors fall upon you, for you will live long alone with the white-headed 'old Ten.' Come with me a little."

Then he dropped my hand, and folded his own behind his bent back, and I followed him slowly along the dusty street. As we were crossing the principal plaza, we met Iu-i-tsaih-ti-e-tsa. She drew her head-mantle over her eyes, and was about to pass us when the governor straightened up, smiled, and greeted her.

"Ha?" inquired the bashful maiden, when he told her something was on his mind.

"Only this," he added: "my little brother will be lonely while I am gone; perhaps he would be less so if you took him a tray of *he-we* once in a while, you know it is 'homesick' to eat alone."

"Ya," assented the girl, as she tripped past us, and we plodded along.

"Now, little brother, stay at home like a man of dignity, while I am gone. Don't you know it is shameless to run all round the streets and over the house-tops as you do? Better your thoughts, and make your heart good, and remember that your brother speaks for you *once more*."

Poor old brother! Good old brother! He never had occasion to mention Iu-i-tsaih-ti-e-tsa to me again, and for many months a shade passed over his face whenever he saw her or heard her name.

We went on past the gardens, and far out into the plain. Then he stopped me.

"Little brother," said he, and he laid one hand on my shoulder, while with the other he removed his head-band, and pressed both of mine, "*This day we have a father who, from his ancient place, rises hard holding his course; grasping us that we may stumble not in the trails of our lives. If it be well, may his grasp be firm until, happily, our paths join together again, and we look one upon the other.* Thus much I make prayer,—I go."

With this he turned suddenly, a tear in his eye, and walked hastily along the river-side. And I stood there watching him, until his bent form disappeared, and trying hard to bear the loneliest moment of all my exile in Zuñi. God bless my Indian brother!

I expected to have a hard time with my "white-headed mother," as I called her; but she was the soul of tenderness and attention. Only one circumstance occurred to jar our peace; that, happily, the second day. I was not in the house when the crash came; but entering soon after, I saw the cause of it, and heard from the mother. Something stood in the middle of my room, with a white mantle of cotton spread over it. I lifted the mantle, and discovered a handsome tray of flaky *he-we*. The mother was awaiting me—much as a spider waits for a fly—just inside the next room.

"Who brought it, mother?" said I, in mock surprise.

"*You* ask who brought it? Well! Who should it be but that shameless wench who lives over the covered way, whose mother has clog feet, and whose father is so poor that no one knows how they live? No matter if young fools do grow crazy over her; she's nothing, nothing at all, Medicine Flower, nothing but a common creature that is not human enough to know what shame is."

A ZUÑI SILVERSMITH.

"Indeed, was it Iu-i-tsaih-ti-e-tsa?"

"Then I knew it!" she rejoined. "You knew all about it. You are not going to let her make a fool of *you*, are you, Medicine Flower? (I was usually her *child*, but on this occasion I was *Medicine Flower*, emphatically pronounced.) She doesn't *near* to you at all; she only thinks of what you have and of your fine buttons."

"Where does she live, mother?"

"Why do you ask?"

"I wish to go and see her."

"I'll have nothing to do with it. Shame myself? Not I!"

"But I wish to *pay* her."

"Ha! my child? Right over the covered way, up two ladders, and down the first sky-hole," replied the old lady, suddenly as bland as though spite had never caused her heart to beat the faster during her long life.

"I'm going to have her come here."

"*No!* She shall not come into——"

"Wait, mother, wait. Have her come here to eat, and then refuse to eat with her, and pay her sugar; but mind, don't you tell my good old brother."

"Your brother? Aha! Then *he* was mixed up in it, was he? Poor child! I thought it was you. So it was Pa-lo-wah-ti-wa. Ah, well! he's a *Pino*, you know—the family is all alike; he belongs to a good clan, but his father's blood is *his* blood."

Peace was made with the mother, and I went to the house of Iu-i-tsaih-ti-e-tsa. She was not at home. I left word for her to come and eat with me at sunset. When she came, I was writing. She was accompanied by her aunt. I bade them enter, set coffee, bread, *he-we*, sugar, and other delicacies before them. Then I merely broke a crust, sacrificed some of it to the fire, ate a mouthful, and left them, resuming my writing. The girl dropped her half-eaten bread, threw her head-mantle over her face, and started for the door. I called to her and offered her a bag of sugar in payment, I said, for the *he-we*. At first she angrily refused; then bethinking herself that I was an American and possibly knew no better, she took the sugar and hastened away, mortified and almost ready to cry with vexation. Poor girl! I knew I was offering her a great dishonor,—as runs the custom of her people,—but it was my only way out of a difficulty far more serious than it could have possibly appeared to her people. The aunt was an old friend of mine. She had frequently come to our house to help grind corn, or make *he-we*, and thought much of me,—calling me, always, *ha-ni* (a sister's younger brother). She remained a few moments; then rising, thanked me, and was about to go when I said to her: "Sister, Iu-i-tsaih-ti-e-tsa is a good and pretty girl. I like her; but it will be many days before I think of women save as sisters and mothers." The woman hesitated a moment, then said:

"Ha-ni, you are a good being, but an unknowable sort of a man. You have caused stance; and I know that of all services I ever did her, such as that ranked in her estimation foremost. It taught me that even "squaws" could sometimes appreciate such attentions.

ZUÑI COURTSHIP.

me to think much this night and made me ashamed, but then!—may you sit happily, even alone," she added, as she passed out of the door.

(However out of place these statements may seem, I deem them not only essential to the narrative, but characteristic of the Zuñis, and of their early attitude toward me. Possibly, too, they may disarm charges and criticisms which are as narrow, unrefined, and malicious, as they are false.)

The old mother entered immediately, and without further remark than a sigh of relief, cleared the things away.

During our lonely life together, I often helped her to split wood, or lift heavy burdens, wind yarn, or bring water. She never failed to thank me for the least of these services. Once she came in, looking tired; I arose and offered her my seat by the hearth. She hesitated a moment, laughed hysterically, then sat down; but in trying to thank me, burst into tears. "Ah!" said she, "*tsa-wai-k'i* (son), don't be so kind to me; I am old." But she never ceased to mention the little circum-

During my lonely life that spring, a few young men fell into the habit of visiting me occasionally, to "hear about the world." They would light their cigarettes, square themselves along the opposite wall, their faces beaming with expectation and satisfaction. An amusing chapter could be written on their questions and comments. I give here but one instance.

One of them asked me, "How the sun could travel so constantly over the world by day and back under it at night, without getting tired and giving it up?"

I explained that the earth revolved and the sun stood still, which caused day and night and made the sun appear to move, illustrating the statement as well as I could; also telling them, that "twice a year the earth wagged back and forth, which made winter come and go and the sun move from one side of Thunder Mountain to the other."

For a few moments they sat still and puffed vigorously at their cigarettes, as thoughtful men are apt to do. Of a sudden, one of them cried out:

"Listen! the Medicine Flower is right. If you gallop past Thunder Mountain, Thunder Mountain moves, and you stand still; and besides, I have noticed that in summer the great hanging snow-bank (Milky Way) drifts from the left of the Land of Daylight (N. E.) to the right of the World of Waters (S. W.); and in winter, from the left of the World of Waters (N. W.) to the right of the Land of Daylight (S. E.). Now! how could they move the great hanging snow-drift without moving the sky too? It would be easier to wag the world than to turn the sky around."

"Ah! but our ancients taught us ——"

"No matter what our ancients taught us," said the young philosopher; "why do you speak the words of dead men? They lied, and Medicine Flower speaks straight, for why should the sun go so far and let the earth stand still, when, by merely rolling her over, he could save himself all that trouble?"

Meanwhile, three times word came from my old brother that he was "homesick for me." Finally he sent a horse, with the message that "if I did not ride it back the next day he should cease to speak to me, believing, that in forgetting him I had found another brother." But when I rode down the neatly tilled and irrigated fields, the old man, who was breaking clods, dropped his hoe, ran up to my side, pulled me from the saddle, embraced me, and that night sat up until nearly daylight, close by my side, in the low room of his quaint farm-house, talking. When time came for me to return, he gave up his work, and with K'ia-wu accompanied me, leaving the fields to the brother-in-law, with whom — K'ia-wu told me delightedly — "peace had been made."

It was well that we returned! The wind-storms were growing worse: day after day they had drifted the scorching sand over the valley, until the springs were choked up and the river was so dry that a stranger could not have distinguished it from a streamless arroyo. The nation was threatened with famine. Many were the grave speculations and councils relative to the "meaning of the gods in thus punishing their children."

Strange to say, I was given a prominent place in these, and was often appealed to, on account of my reputed "knowledge of the world." More and more frequent and desperate grew these gatherings, until at last a poor fellow named "Big Belly" was seized and brought up before them, accused of "heresy!" The trial — in which I had taken no part — lasted a whole day and part of night, when to my surprise a body of elders summoned me, and placed me at the head of their council. They addressed and treated me as chief counselor of their nation, which office I held thenceforward for nearly two years. Among other things, they asked what should be done. I inquired minutely into the case, and learned that the culprit had opened one of the sand-choked springs, which proved to be sacred. The gods were supposed to be angry with the nation on account of his transgression,— demanding the sacrifice of his life. As impassionately as possible, I pleaded that the wind-storms had set in long before he opened the spring, and suggested that he be made to fill it up again and to sacrifice bits of shells and turquois to it. The suggestion was adopted! The additional penalty of ostracism, however, was laid upon him; and to this day he lives in the farming pueblo of K'iap-kwai-na-kwin, or Ojo Caliente.

One evil followed another. Many deaths occurred, among them, that of a beautiful girl, who had been universally liked. Nor did the wind-storms abate. As a consequence, I heard one night a peculiar, long war-cry. It was joined by another and another, until the sound grew strangely weird and ominous. Then three or four men rushed past my door yelling: "A wizard! a wizard!" The tribe was soon in an uproar. The priests of the Bow had seized an old man named the "Bat," and in one of their secret chambers were trying him for sorcery. I was not present, of course, at the trial; but at three o'clock in the morning they dragged him forth to the hill on the north side of the pueblo. There they tied his hands behind him with a rawhide rope; and passing the end of the latter over a pole, supported by high crotched posts, they drew him up until his toes barely touched the ground and he was bent almost double.

Then the four chief-priests of the Bow approached and harangued him one by one, but provoked no reply save the most piteous moans. Day dawned; yet still he hung there. The speeches grew louder and more furious, until, fearing violence, I ran home, buckled on my pistol, and returned. I went straight to the old man's side.

"Go back," said the accusers.

"I will not go back; for I come with words."

"Speak them," said they.

"These," said I. "You may try the old man, but you must not kill him. The Americans will see you, or find it out, and tell their people, who will say: 'The Zuñis murdered one of their own grandfathers.' That will bring trouble on you all."

"What! murder a wizard?" they exclaimed. "Ho!" and for a few moments I grew hopeless; for the chief-priest turned to the old man, and asked, with mock tenderness ·

"Father, does it hurt?"

"Ai-o," moaned the old man, in a weak voice. "I die, I am dying."

"That's right," retorted the priest. "Pull him up a little higher, my son," said he, addressing an assistant. "He says it hurts, and I have hopes he will speak." Then he turned to me again.

"This is our way, my son, of bringing bad men to wisdom; I have worn my throat out urging him to speak; now I am trying another way. If he but speak, he shall be let to go."

"What shall I say?" piteously moaned the suffering man.

"Say *yes* or NO! dotard," howled the priest.

"Speak, grandfather, speak!" said I, as re-assuringly as I could, at the same time laying my hand on his withered arm.

"Tell them to let me down, then," he pleaded, "for I can speak not long as I am; I shall die. Oh! I shall die."

"Thanks! father, thanks!" said the priest, briskly. "Let him down; he is coming to his senses, I see."

They let the sufferer down for a moment; and gazing on the ground, he began:

"True! I have been bad. My father taught me fifty years ago, in the mountains of the summer snows. It was medicine that I used. You will find a bundle of it over the rafters, in my highest room."

One of the attendants was immediately dispatched, and soon returned with a little bunch of twigs.

"Ay! that it is, I used that. It has covered me with shame; but I will be better. I will rejoin my *ti-k'ia* (sacred order). It will surely rain within four days; for if you but let me go, I shall join my *ti-k'ia* again."

"Will you be wise?"

"Yes! believe me."

"Will you stay in Zuñi?"

"Yes! believe me."

"Will you never more cause tears?"

"No! It were a shame."

"Will you never teach to others your magic?"

"No! believe me——"

"Thanks! You have spoken. Let him go!" said the priest, as he walked hastily through the crowd toward his home.

Four days passed, and no rain came; nor did the "Bat" do as he had promised, for he returned home only to threaten revenge on the priesthood, and since the fifth day no one outside of that priesthood has ever seen a trace of the "Bat."

In Zuñi law-custom there are but two crimes punishable by death—sorcery and cowardice in battle. If, however, a man attempt the life of another, or even threaten it, he is regarded as a wizard; but no immediate measures are taken for his correction. Should crops fail, wind-storms prevail, or should the threatened man die, even from natural causes, the reputed wizard is, when he least expects it, dragged from his bed at night by the secret council of the A-pi-thlan-shi-wa-ni, taken to their chamber and tried long and fairly. Should the culprit persist in silence, he is taken forth and tortured by the simple yet excruciatingly painful method I have described, throughout a "single course of the sun"; and if still silent, again taken to the chamber of the priesthood, whence he never comes forth alive; nor do others than members of the dread organization ever know what becomes of him. Rare indeed is the execution for which no other than superstitious reasons may be adduced. Even in case of the "Bat," I learned that he had attempted to poison his own niece, the girl heretofore mentioned, the death of whom, a few weeks afterward, rendered him a criminal and liable to condemnation, not only as such, but as a sorcerer. Thus, like a vigilance committee, the priesthood of the Bow secretly tries all cases of capital crime under the name of sorcery or witchcraft,—the war-chief of the nation, himself necessarily a prominent priest of the Bow, acting as executioner, and, with the aid of his sub-chiefs, as secretly disposing of the body. On account of this mysterious method of justice crime is rare in Zuñi.

At last, in late June, rains came. As if by magic, the dust-storms ceased, and the plains were overspread with bright green. The Zuñis became uproariously happy. The members of the little "bees," that were formed for mutual assistance in the field labors, laughed and joked at their work from sunrise till supper-time. The river flowed broad and clear again. Thither again flocked the urchin population as I had seen them the autumn before.

One day I saw some of the children playing at "breaking horses." One juvenile demon was leading a band of four or five others, in the pursuit of a big bristling boar. Lasso in hand, the little fellow watched his chance, and, twirling the flexible cord once or twice rapidly in the air, sent it like lightning toward the head of the boar. The latter made a desperate dash only to run his snout and forefoot into the coil, which, held by the combined efforts of all, quickly precipitated him, in a succession of entangling somersaults, into the shallow river. In an instant another lasso was dexterously thrown over his hind feet, and his captors, heedless of mud and water, wild with

TORTURING A SORCERER.

vociferous glee, bestraddled him, and held him down. The leader tore off one of the legs of his cotton trowsers, and with this he bandaged the eyes of the squealing animal, wrapping another piece tightly around his snout so as to smother his cries. Thus equipped, the hog was set at liberty. Two of the little wretches jumped astride him, while the others prodded him behind and at the sides. Thus goaded, the poor beast ran uncertainly in all directions, into corrals, over logs, headlong into deep holes, precipitating his adventuresome riders; not, however, to their discomfiture, for they would immediately scamper up, drive, push, lead, or haul him out, and mount him again. The last I saw of them was toward evening; they were ruefully regarding the dead carcass of their novel horse.

With midsummer the heat became intense. My brother and I sat, day after day, in the cool under-rooms of our house,—the latter busy with his quaint forge and crude appliances, working Mexican coins over into bangles, girdles, ear-rings, buttons, and what not, for savage adornment. Though his tools were wonderfully rude, the work he turned out by dint of combined patience and ingenuity was remarkably beautiful. One day as I sat watching him, a procession of fifty men went hastily down the hill, and off westward over the plain. They were solemnly led by a painted and shell-bedecked priest, and followed by the torch-bearing Shu-lu-wit-si, or God of Fire. After they had vanished, I asked old brother what it all meant.

"They are going," said he, "to the city of the Ka-ka and the home of our others."

Four days after, toward sunset, costumed and masked in the beautiful paraphernalia of the Ka-k'ok-shi, or "Good Dance," they returned in file up the same pathway, each bearing in his arms a basket filled with living, squirming turtles, which he regarded and carried as tenderly as a mother would her infant. Some of the wretched reptiles were carefully wrapped in soft blankets, their heads and forefeet protruding,—and, mounted on the backs of the plume-bedecked pilgrims, made ludicrous but solemn caricatures of little children in the same position.

While I was at supper upstairs, that evening, the governor's brother-in-law came in. He was welcomed by the family as if a messenger from heaven. He bore in his tremulous fingers one of the much-abused and rebellious turtles. Paint still adhered to his hands and bare feet, which led me to infer that he had formed one of the sacred embassy.

"So you went to Ka-thlu-el-lon, did you?" I asked.

"E'e," replied the weary man, in a voice husky with long chanting, as he sank, almost exhausted, on a roll of skins which had

THE DEMON OF CHILDHOOD.

been placed for him, and tenderly laid the turtle on the floor. No sooner did the creature find itself at liberty than it made off as fast as its lame legs would take it. Of one accord, the family forsook dish, spoon, and drinking-cup, and grabbing from a sacred meal-bowl whole handfuls of the contents, hurriedly followed the turtle about the room, into dark corners, around water-jars, behind the grinding-troughs, and out into the middle of the floor again, praying and scattering meal on its back as they went. At last, strange to say, it approached the foot-sore man who had brought it.

"Ha!" he exclaimed, with emotion; "see, it comes to me again; ah, what great favors the fathers of all grant me this day," and passing his hand gently over the sprawling animal, he inhaled from his palm deeply and long, at the same time invoking the favor of the gods. Then he leaned his chin upon his hand, and with large, wistful eyes regarded his ugly captive as it sprawled about blinking its meal-bedimmed eyes, and clawing the smooth floor in memory of its native element. At this juncture, I ventured a question:

"Why do you not let him go, or give him some water?"

Slowly the man turned his eyes toward

A ZUÑI BURIAL.

me, an odd mixture of pain, indignation, and pity on his face, while the worshipful family stared at me with holy horror.

"Poor younger brother!" he said, at last; "know you not how precious it is? It die? It will *not* die; I tell you, it *cannot* die."

"But it will die if you don't feed it and give it water."

"I tell you it *cannot* die; it will only change houses to-morrow, and go back to the home of its brothers. Ah, well! How should *you* know?" he mused. Turning to the blinded turtle again: "Ah! my poor dear lost child or parent, my sister or brother to have been! Who knows which? May be my own great-grand-father or mother!" And with this he fell to weeping most pathetically, and, tremulous with sobs, which were echoed by the women and children, he buried his face in his hands. Filled with sympathy for his grief, however mistaken, I raised the turtle to my lips and kissed its cold shell; then depositing it on the floor, hastily left the grief-stricken family to their sorrows.

Next day, with prayers and tender beseechings, plumes and offerings, the poor turtle was killed, and its flesh and bones were removed and deposited in the little river, that it might "return once more to eternal life among its comrades in the dark waters of the lake of the dead." The shell, carefully scraped and dried, was made into a dance-rattle, and, covered by a piece of buckskin, it still hangs from the smoke-stained rafters of my brother's house.

Once a Navajo tried to buy it for a ladle; loaded with indignant reproaches, he was turned out of the house. Were any one to venture the suggestion that the turtle no longer lived, his remark would cause a flood of tears, and he would be reminded that it had only "changed houses and had gone to live forever in the home of 'our lost others.'"

This persistent adherence to the phrase, "our lost others," struck me as significant. Had they believed in the transmigration of the soul, they would have said "our brothers, our fathers, our children," I reasoned; and yet it was long before I learned the true meaning of it. At last, a wonderful epic, including the genesis and sacred history of the Zuñi ancestry, was repeated in my hearing by an old blind priest, through which I came to understand the regard my adopted people had for the turtle. I give a portion of the tradition as afterward explained to me:

"In the days of the new, after the times when all mankind had come forth from one to the other of the 'four great cavern wombs of earth' *(a-wi-ten te-huthl-na-kwin)*, and had come out into the light of our father, the sun, they journeyed, under the guidance of A-hai-iu-ta and Ma-tsai-le-ma, twin children of the sun, immortal youths, toward the father of all men and things, eastward.

"In those times, a day meant four years, and a night the same; so that, in the speech of the ancients, 'Between one sunrise and another' means eight years.

"After many days and nights, the people settled

near the mountain of the Medicine Flower, and a great cazique sent forward his two children, a young man and a young girl, — the passing beautiful of all children, — to explore for a better country. When they had journeyed as far as the region where now flow the red waters [Colorado Chiquito], they paused to rest from their journey. Ah! they sinned and were changed to a demon god and goddess.

"The world was damp. Plant corn on the mountain-tops, and it grew. Dig a hole into the sands at will, and water filled it.

"The woman in her anger drew her foot through the sands, that she might—from shame—separate herself from her people; and the waters, collecting, flowed off until they were a deep channel; yet they settled most about the place where she stood, and it became a lake which is there to this day. And the mark in the sands is the valley where now flow the red waters.

"No tidings came from the young messengers; and after many days the nation again journeyed eastward, carrying upon their backs not only their things precious, but also their little children. When they reached the waters they were dismayed; but some ventured in to cross over. Fear filled the hearts of many mothers, for their children grew cold and strange, like others than human creatures, and they dropped them into the waters, changed indeed; they floated away, crying and moaning, as ever now they cry and moan when the night comes on and the hunter camps near their shores. But those who loved their children and were strong of heart passed safely over the flood and found them the same as before.

"*Thus* it came to be that only part of our nation ever arrived at the 'middle of the world.' But it is well, as all things are; for others were left to remember us and to make a home, not of strangers, but of 'our others,' for those who should die and to intercede with the 'Holders of the Waters of the World' that all mankind and unfinished creatures, even flying and creeping beings, might have food to eat and water to drink when the world should harden and the land should dry up. And in that lake is a descending ladder, down which even the smallest may enter fearlessly, who has passed its borders in death; where it is delightful, and filled with songs and dances; where all men are brothers, and whence they wander whither they will, to minister to and guide those whom they have left behind them—that is the lake where live 'our others' and whither go our dead. At night, he who wanders on the hills of the Ka-ko'k-shi may sometimes see the light shining forth and hear strange voices of music coming up from the depths of those waters."

For the Zuñi, therefore, there is a city of the living and another of the dead. As the living may wander through far countries, so may the dead return to their birthland, or pass over from one ocean to another.

Possibly, at some remote period, the ancestors of the Zuñis have believed in the transmigration of the soul, of which belief these particular superstitions relative to the turtle remain as survivals. Their belief to-day, however, relative to the future life is spiritualistic. As illustrative of this and of their funeral customs, I conclude with an account of the death and burial, toward the close of my first year among them, of my adopted uncle.

For more than a year he had been wasting with consumption, when, on account of a medical reputation which had greatly aided me and had, indeed, given rise to my name, I was called to see him. I gave him such simple remedies as I had at hand, and he became very fond of me, at last adopting me as his nephew, and naming me Hai-iu-tsaih-ti-wa.

Toward the last, the old man talked often of his approaching death, speaking of the future life with an amount of conviction which surprised me.

"To dwell with my relatives, even those whose names were wasted before my birth, is that painful to the thought?" said the old man. "Often, when we dream not, yet we see and hear them as in dreams." "A man is like a grain of corn—bury him, and he molds; yet his heart lives, and springs out on the breath of life [the soul] to make him as he was, so again."

He grew rapidly feebler. For two or three days I did not see him. Hearing that he was worse, I hastened to his side. He was unconscious, and a crowd of relatives were thickly gathered around him, wringing their hands and wailing. Presently he opened his eyes.

"Hush," said he, and he raised his hand weakly with a smile of recognition, not of me, but of something he seemed to see. Then he turned to me. "My boy, I *thought* you would come," he murmured. "Now I can bid you, 'I go'; for they are — all around me — and I know— they have come for me—*this* time. My heart makes happy. *No*," said he, as a medicine-man tried to force breath into his mouth. "No, I go not alone! Let me go! *E-lu-ia* (Delightful!)"

Then he closed his eyes and became unconscious again, smiling even in his dying sleep.

Two hours after, the women of the same clan which had sprinkled water and meal on him when a baby, adopting him as "their child of the sun," bathed his body and broke a vessel of water by its side, thus renouncing all claim to him forever and returning his being to the sun. Then four men took the blanket-roll by the corners and carried it, amid the mourning wails of the women, to the ancient burial-place. They hastily lowered it into a shallow grave, while one standing to the east said a prayer, scattered meal, food, and other offerings upon it; then they as hastily covered it over, clearing away all traces of the new-made grave. *Now* I know not the bone-strewn grave of "my uncle" from those of a thousand others, for the "silent majority" of the Zuñi nation lie in the same small square. Four days later, down by the river, a little group of mourners sacrificed, with beseeching in the name of the dead, the only flowers their poor land affords—the beautiful prayer-plumes of the "birds of summerland."

Frank H. Cushing.

AN ABORIGINAL PILGRIMAGE

The Zuñi Indians, of New Mexico and Arizona, are now a mere handful of people, but in their keeping is a wonderful history, which perpetuates an ancient cultus related to that of the Toltecs, the Aztecs, and the Incas. Mr. Frank H. Cushing, of the Smithsonian Institute, who by living among them has made a great gain for ethnological learning, will contribute to this magazine an account of his unique experiences. Our present purpose is to give an account of the remarkable pilgrimage of a number of the chief men of Zuñi to "the Ocean of Sunrise." For many years, it had been the dream of some of these men to visit the East, which was to them a land of fable. Tales of its marvels, incredible because inconceivable, from time to time had drifted to them. "The Apaches are bad, but they have been to Washington; the Navajos have been to Washington; all Indians have been to Washington but the still-sitting ones," said the Zuñis. The motives that prompted the expedition were various. On Mr. Cushing's part there was, first of all, the advancement of his work by strengthening the ties between the people and himself; and second, the good of the people by arousing them to a desire for education and advancement through what was to be seen in the East. With the Indian pilgrims the reasons were more complex. At their first council upon the subject, Nai-iu-tchi, the senior priest of the Order of the Bow, into which Mr. Cushing had been initiated the previous autumn, declared that whoever else was to be chosen he certainly must go; and he advanced what was agreed to be the most important of the reasons for undertaking the trip—namely, to bring back to Zuñi sacred water from "the Ocean of Sunrise" or "the Waters of the World of Day."

The primary reason for taking the "water that brings rain, and the water of the sacred medicine altar," as the Zuñi term it, from the Atlantic Ocean was the position of the latter with reference to the sun. Nai-iu-tchi promised—Mr. Cushing entrance into the Order of the Kâ-kâ as a reward for the great service of conducting them to the ocean. Otherwise entrance could not have been obtained without marriage into the tribe. The Zuñis say that their gods brought them to a dry and sterile country for a home, but that their forefathers taught them the prayers and songs whereby that land might be blessed with rain. They therefore addressed their prayers to the spirits dwelling in the ocean, the home of all water, as the source from which their blessing came. They believe their prayers brought the clouds from the ocean, guided by the spirits of their ancestors, and the clouds gave the rain. These prayers could not be efficacious, however, without the help of a drop of ocean water to start them aright.

The Zuñis have had a knowledge of the oceans from time immemorial, and, besides the Atlantic and the "Ocean of Hot Water," (the Gulf of Mexico), they speak of the "Ocean of Sunset" and the "Ocean of the Place of Everlasting Snow," and they include all four under the name of "The waters embracing the world." When asked how it was that they knew all about the ocean, one of them said to the writer: "Farther back than a long time ago, our fathers told their children about the ocean of sunrise. We ourselves did not know it. We had not seen it. We knew it in the prayers they had taught us, and by the things they had handed down to us, and which came from its waters."

At the council, when Nai-iu-tchi was told that he had been chosen to go, he repeated the ancient Zuñi tradition of the people that had gone to the eastward in the days when all mankind was one, and said that now "Our Lost Others," as they were called, might be coming back to meet them in the shape of the Americans. The councils now were filled with talk about the Americans, and all the traditions, reports, and rumors ever heard about them were repeated over and over again. Among these was one of the first accounts that had ever been brought to Zuñi concerning us, and it ran thus: "A strange and unknown people are the Americans, and in a far-off and unknown land live they. Thus said Our Old Ones. It is said that they are white, with short hair, and that they touch not their food with their fingers, but eat with fingers and knives of iron, and talk much while eating." At last it was decided who were to form the party. Ki-ä-si or Ki-ä-si-wa, the junior priest of the Order of the Bow, was to accompany his colleague; but only after protracted discussion, for it was firmly believed that, should these two priests by any accident not be back in time for the important ceremonies of the summer solstice, some great catastrophe would befall the entire nation. The other Zuñis chosen for the party were Pa-lo-wah-ti-wa, the governor, or political head-chief of Zuñi, and Mr. Cushing's brother by adoption; Lai-iu-ai-tsai-lu, or Pedro Piño, as he is commonly known, the father of Pa-lo-wah-ti-wa, and formerly governor of Zuñi for thirty years, now a wrinkled old man of between eighty and ninety years; Lai-iu-ah-tsai-lun-k'ia, the priest of the temple

FRANK H. CLUSHING

and Mr. Cushing's father by adoption; and, finally, Na-na-he, a Moqui who had been adopted into the nation by marriage, a youthful-looking man of thirty-five years, and a member of the Order of the Lesser Fire.

At last the day for departure came, February 22, 1882. Before the Governor's house out-door services were held for the entire population, and the pilgrims were prayed over by the assembled priesthood within. With each there were the parting formalities of an embrace, heart to heart, hand in hand, and breath to breath. Just before the start, Nai-iu-tchi ascended to the house-top and blessed the multitude in a loud voice. The first night they encamped at the piñon-covered foothills beyond the summer *pueblo* of Las Nutrias. They arrived at Fort Wingate the next afternoon. In the evening Mr. Cushing exchanged the picturesque Zuñi costume, which had been his garb for nearly three years, for the dress of civilization. The question of his wearing "American clothes" on the trip had been a serious one with the Zuñis, and it was a subject of many deliberations. Assent was given only on the representation that it would displease his brothers the Americans should he not do it, their feeling for conventionality in dress being as strong as that of the Zuñis. This motive was one that appealed to them forcibly and was readily understood.

When they arrived at the railway station the next morning, they stood close beside the track as the locomotive came up, and though three of them, Pedro Piño, Ki-ä-si, and Na-na-he, had never seen a locomotive, they never flinched. As they settled into their seats in the passenger-coach they breathed a long sigh of gratitude, followed by their exclamation of thanksgiving, "*E-ah kwa!*" When the train started they raised the window-sash and prayed aloud, each scattering a pinch of their prayer-meal, composed of corn-meal with an admixture of finely ground precious sea-shells, which they always carried with them in little bags.

During the afternoon they passed the *pueblo* of Laguna, at the sight of which they marveled greatly, saying: "Can it be that the sun has stood still in the heavens? For here in these few hours we have come to a place to reach which it used to take us three days upon our fleetest ponies! "And when at sundown they passed the *pueblo* of Isleta on the Rio Grande, their wonder was greater still. For the next three days they kept pretty closely on board the train, taking their meals in the baggage-car. They had brought with them great quantities of Zuñi food, for fear that they might not like the American diet. It proved afterward that they liked many articles of our *cuisine,* but the variety was too much for them. They thought that the Americans ate too many things and "dared their insides." One of them said one day:

"My inside is not only filled with food, but also

with much fighting."

On the second day of the journey, the chief engineer of the Atchison, Topeka, and Santa Fé Railroad, who was on the train, wanted Mr. Cushing to take one of the Indians on the locomotive. Nai-iu-tchi, who was always ready for anything, was selected. He stood unmoved while the whistle was blown at its shrillest, and regarding reverently the action of the locomotive, he exclaimed:

"The Americans are gods, only they have to eat material food!"

They were deeply interested in the farms that lined the railroad and wondered at their great number, and were struck by the increasing number and size of the rivers as they proceeded eastward, greeting every new body of water with prayers. One day on the train they talked incessantly about their

PEDRO PIÑO. LAI-IU-AM-TSAI-LA. FORMERLY GOVERNOR OF ZUÑI FOR THIRTY YEARS.

leader, both to him and among themselves. The burden of their talk was what a great man Té-na-tsa-li was; everything had turned out as he bad said it would be, and they begged his pardon that they had not fully believed him in Zuñi, not deeming it possible that such wonders as he had described could exist. It showed that the Americans were truthful pcoplc, thcy said, and not liars like the Navajos.

At Quincy there was a long wait for the connecting train of the Chicago, Burlington, and Quincy Railroad, and the conductor who had come with them from Kansas City invited the party to comic up into the square with him. This was the first American city into which they had been, and they looked excitedly from one thing to another, each seeing something different and all talking at once, like pleased children.

At the hotel in Chicago they essayed their first meal in American fashion, making laughable attempts with their knives and forks, which the most of them used for the first time. But they were determined to do as the Americans did while in their land, and to honor their customs. At the water-tower in Chicago they were awe-struck in the presence of the mighty engine, and became vexed with Mr. Cushing because he prevented them from touching it, as they wished to, in every part, even where the action was most swift and powerful, with the thought

PORTRAIT AND AUTOGRAPH OF NAI-JU-TCHI, SENIOR PRIEST, ORDER OF THE BOW, CLAN OF THE EAGLES, SUN AND RATTLESNAKE, EMBLEMS OF HIS ORDERS.

THE "SONG." ZUÑI AT PAINT-AND-CLAY CLUB.

thus to absorb its influence. "What if it should hurt us? It would nevertheless be all right, and just about as it should be!" said they, with their strange fatalism. They prayed before the engine, but not to it, as might have been supposed by some; their prayers were addressed to the god through whom the construction of such a mighty work was made possible.

Chicago-Quin., as they termed it, they called a city of *pueblos*. They said their hotel was a *pueblo* in itself, and they wondered if each of the large blocks of buildings was the dwelling place of a separate clan of Chicagoans.

Driving through one of the parks they saw two sea-lions, or walruses, which were kept there. Recognizing that they were ocean animals, they almost broke their drivers' arms in their impetuous haste to stop the carriages. They ran up to the animals, exclaiming: "At last, after long waiting, we greet ye, O our fathers!" considering them as "animal gods of the ocean," and began praying most fervently, first forcing a portion of prayer-meal into Té-na-tsa-li's hand. When they came in sight of the lake they could hardly be made to believe that it was not the ocean, and, until convinced that it was fresh water, they wanted to make their sacrifices and perform their ceremonies.

It was night when they arrived in Washington, and when told that they were there at last they repeatedly stretched their hands out into the evening air, drawing them to their lips and inhaling, thus absorbing the sacred influence of the place. Arrived at the hotel Mr. Cushing broached to his companions the subject of cutting his hair, which was eighteen inches long, and which was making him unpleasantly conspicuous. His *caciques* desired it, he said, and it would gratify his brothers the Americans, and show them that the Zuñis were considerate of their wishes. The Zuñis could not see how it was that the Americans objected to long hair, which was the crowning glory of a man. They were slow in consenting and could only be made to at last by the promise from Mr. Cushing that he would have it made up, so that he could wear it beneath his head-band when back at Zuñi, "for," said they, "no one could become a member of the Kâ-kâ without long hair."

The Zuñis were highly gratified at their reception by President Arthur. Old Pedro Piño was moved to tears at thus "grasping the hand of Washington," which was the crowning event of his life, but his emotion was not so great as at the tomb of Washington, where he wept uncontrollably. The name of Washington was to him connected with the old army officers for whom he had such an affection years before. The old man took a severe chill on the steam-boat going down the Potomac. In his gallantry he refused to leave some ladies who were on deck, and the raw March air was too much for him. But he insisted that at the tomb of Washington, "while he was engaged in prayer, his heart wept until his thoughts decayed," and that was why be was made sick. He was too feeble to undertake the trip to Boston, and he was therefore left at the home of one of the stanchest friends of the Zuñis, Mr. James

PORTRAIT AND AUTOGRAPH OF KI-A-SI, JUNIOR PRIEST, ORDER OF THE BOW, CLAN OF THE BADGERS.

Stevenson, Mr. Cushing's colleague at the Bureau of Ethnology, and one of the bravest Rocky Mountain explorers of the Geological Survey. It was with Mr. Stevenson's expedition in 1879 that Mr. Cushing went to Zuñi. With Mr. and Mrs. Stevenson old Pedro quickly adapted himself to civilized ways, and even insisted on using a finger-bowl at the table. The old man's iron will was wonderful. One day, after the return of the others from Boston, his son, the Governor, took a notion while strolling out to climb the Washington Monument. He said that he went "up and up and up until his thighs said no," and his semihumorous account of what he saw from the summit— "no longer the powerful Americans, but little men like ants creeping around on the ground below, and horses no larger than mice, and instead of the great Potomac, a little stream hardly larger than the Zuñi River,"—all this so excited the curiosity of the old fellow that the next day he went quietly out and made the climb himself. It exhausted him so that he could scarcely move, but he was all right again in twenty-four hours.

The ocean ceremony was to be performed at Boston on account of the desire of the Zuñis to get the water as far to the eastward as possible, and because of the interest felt in Mr. Cushing's work by his scientific friends there and in Cambridge. The journey through New England was by daylight, and there were so many streams to pass that before the Indians could put away their bags of prayer-meal they would be required again. Praying was therefore almost incessant.

Their first social experience was at the Paint-and-Clay Club, which thus reciprocated the hospitality shown two of its members at Zuñi the previous summer. It was a most picturesque evening, and the scene was one to delight both civilized and barbarous eyes. The ruddy walls glowed a cheery welcome, and two great high-reliefs upon them—the heads of an Indian and a Norseman, typical of the original possessors and discoverers of our soil—looked approvingly down. The Indians peered curiously about, exploring nooks and corners, and when they saw the terra-cotta model of one of Barye's tigers, they formed a reverent group and prayed. The striking faces and brilliant native costumes of the Indians, almost wholly of articles made by themselves—beautifully woven serape shirts, deer-skin knee-breeches, and leggings adorned with rows of close-set silver buttons, moccasins and massive silver belts, necklaces of shell, coral, and turquoise —captivated the artists' eyes, and sketch-books and pencils were in use all

THE FIRST SIGHT OF THE ATLANTIC, AT BOSTON.

the evening. The Governor, with his strong profile, was particularly in favor as a subject.

During their stay a thronged reception was held in the historic "Old South" Meetinghouse, and Mr. Cushing told about Zuñi customs, history, and mythology, while the Indians sang and danced. In one of the folk-lore stories he related there was a passage showing what seems to be an inherent knowledge of one of the great facts of the geological history of their country. It was a story of a young man who followed the spirit of his dead bride. He pursued her over the plains and mountains until he came to a cañon between two mesas, or table-lands. *Now, since the spirit of the earth was there,* the spirit crossed over, but the young man, being mortal, could not pass. Science tells us that the top of the mesas was the ancient level of the country, which has been reduced by the action of the elements, and this the Zuñi also appear to know. All stories seemed to show the intrinsic gentleness of the Zuñi faith, marked though it was by certain cruel and barbarous practices. A cardinal principle appeared to be that even evil things will ultimately become good, their very badness being an instrument to the attainment of that end.

One evening was spent at Wellesley College, with which the Indians were greatly pleased. "E-lu!" (enchantingly beautiful) was their constant exclamation, "What love must the Americans bear their children to send them so far away from home that they may become finished people!" they remarked, and they dwelt on the beauty of the place and its surroundings, of the hundreds of pretty things there, of their "little land of summer" (the conservatory), and when the time for the train came they could hardly be dragged away.

They were taken to see the negro minstrels one night by invitation of Mayor Green, who took a deep interest in Mr. Cushing's work. At first they were enthusiastic over the clog-dancing and various other

PORTRAIT AND AUTOGRAPH OF PA-LO-WAH-TI-WA, GOAVERNOR OF ZUÑI, OR HEAD POLITICAL CHIEF. CLAN OF THE MACAWS.

feats, and expressed themselves in peculiar shrill cries of approbation. But suddenly they became silent, for they conceived the idea that they were witnessing the mysterious rites of one of the secret orders of America, and they therefore repeatedly stretched out their arms to draw in the spirit of the "holy men" upon the stage.

A memorable day was spent at Harvard University. A visit to the Peabody Museum of Archaeology resulted in the discovery by Mr. Cushing of a close relation between the religion of the Incas of Peru and that of the Zuñis. That afternoon there was an athletic tournament by the Harvard students in the gymnasium, at which the Indians were fairly beside themselves with delight at the performances. They maintained that the students must be members of a grand "order of the Elks," an athletic order of the Zuñis, since to achieve such skill they must surely be inspired by the gods.

After a short acquaintance the marked individuality of each Indian was noticeable. The Governor's grave face would occasionally light up with an expressive smile, betraying a decided feeling for humor. Nai-iu-tchi had a genial, contemplative look, a kindly placidity of countenance, and he was full of poetry, telling folk-lore stories charmingly. Ki-ä-si was of a stern, ascetic nature. Old Lai-iu-ah-tsai-lun-k'ia was characterized by extreme amiability and reflectiveness, and the striking resemblance of his profile to that of Dante was frequently spoken of. Na-na-be was a great favorite with the ladies.

They had a way of giving names to people with whom they were often in contact. A reporter who was constantly with them they called O-ma-tsa-pa, the Little Sunflower, which with them is an emblem of smiling cheerfulness. Three of Mr. Cushing's

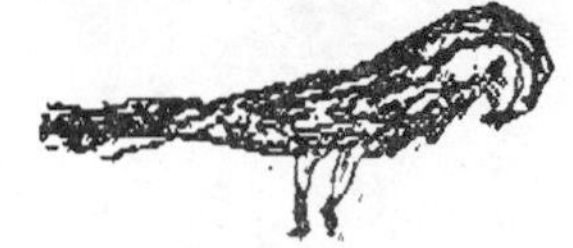

PORTRAIT AND AUTOGRAPH OF LAI-IU-AH-TSAI-LUN-K'IA, PRIEST OF THE TEMPLE, OR MEDICINE CACIQUE. CLAN OF THE PARROTS.

friends, of whom they saw a good deal, were adopted formally, two by Nai-iu-tchi, and one by Lai-iu-ah-tsai-lun-k'ia. The names given them were K'ia-u-lo-ki (the Great Swallow), O-nok-thli-k'ia (the Great Dance Plume), and Thlí-a-kwa (the Blue Medicine Stone, or Turquoise), all names of great honor, being those of sacred objects. The following was the prayer said by Nai-iu-tchi on the adoption of the last:

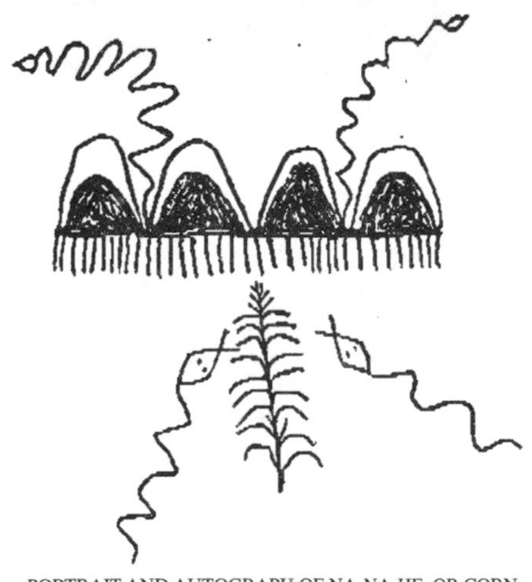

PORTRAIT AND AUTOGRAPH OF NA-NA-HE, OR CORN-FLOWER, MOQUI, MEMBER OF LITTLE FIRE ORDER IN ZUÑI, RATTLESNAKE ORDER IN MOQUI.

"My child! This day I take you in my arms and clasp you strongly, and if it be well, then our father the sun will, in his road over the world, rise, reach his zenith, hold himself firmly, and smile upon you and me that our roads of life may be finished. Hence I grasp you by the hand with the bands and hearts of the gods. I add to thy wind of life, that our roads of life may be finished together. My child, may the light of the gods meet you! My child, *Thlí-a-kwa*."

They visited Salem on the invitation of Professor E. S. Morse, and inspected his collection of Japanese articles. For Japanese art they had conceived a great veneration, saying that in one respect another people excelled the Americans—the art of making things beautiful to the eye. They here found many astonishing similarities to objects of their own mythology; among them the Great Swallow of the Sky, and their sacred turtles. The latter led them to mention a particularly revered mythological animal with them—the turtle with hair on his back; and great was their wonder when a Japanese representation of one was straightway produced.

They had been told of the persecution of the witches at Salem, and as witchcraft is a capital crime in Zuñi, they heartily commended the work, and said that it was on account of the energetic steps taken in those times that the Americans were prosperous to-day, and rid of the curse of witchery. At the public reception held for them in Salem, when told they were in the famous city of the witches, they fell into an animated discussion of the matter among themselves there on the platform. Ki-ä-si, when invited to address the audience, preached a little sermon on witchcraft, which would have pleased old Cotton Mather himself. He thanked the good people of Salem for the service they had done the world, and gave them some advice how to deal with witchcraft should it ever trouble them again. "Be the witches or wizards your dearest relatives or friends, consider not your own hearts," said he, "but remember your duty and spare them not; put them to death!"

They had been in Boston several days, and had not yet seen the ocean. One morning they were taken up into the tower of a lofty building. They stretched out their arms in adoration, and scattered their sacred meal. When the silence was broken, old Nai-iu-tchi exclaimed: "It is all as Our Old Ones said, and as I knew I should find it. The blueblack line out there is the ocean, and the marks of white are the foam it throws up when it is angry." They looked over the sea of buildings spreading out uninterruptedly, far beyond the city limits, and said: "See, on one side the ocean; on the other a world of houses—the great *pueblo* of Boston!"

After a week of sight-seeing, the day set for the rites at the sea-side arrived. It had been a week of chilly March weather, with rain and gray skies, fog, sleet, and few hours of sunshine, so that the Zuñis gave Boston the name of "the City of Perpetual Mists." It was, however, a fortunate city in their eyes to be blessed with so much moisture. In the afternoon, a special steamer took on board a company invited by the mayor and started for Deer Island. The Indians were given seats in the large pilot-house. As the boat sped out into the harbor the Indians fell at once to praying, and did not look up until the boat had nearly reached Deer Island.

Here a tent had been provided, and in this the Indians and Mr. Cushing costumed themselves for the ceremonial in accordance with their sacred ranks in the various orders of the tribe. Nai-iu-tchi, the senior priest of the Bow and traditional priest of the Temple, was distinguished by a small bunch of feathers tied to his hair, over the crown of the head, composed like those of the plume-sticks sacrificed at the summer solstice, with added plumes to the gods of the ocean, or priest-god makers of the "roads of life." He—with the other three members of the Order of the Bow, Ki-ä-si, Pa-lo-wah-ti-wa, and Mr. Cushing was distinguished by bands and spots of a kind of plumbago filled with shining particles upon the face—the war-paint of the Zuñis, and probably representing the twinkling stars, which are the gods of war. Lai-iu-ah-tsai-lun-k'ia wore a plume like Nai-iu-tchi's, with an added white plume as medicine priest of the Order of the Little Fire. His only paint was a faint streak of yellow, the color of the Kâ-kâ. Ki-ä-si wore upon his war-bonnet his plume of membership in the Order of the Bow, and an eagle-feather as a member of the Order of Coyotes or Hunters. All the members of the Bow wore across their shoulders their buckskin badges of rank, and the two priests of the order carried war-clubs, bows, quivers, and emblematic shields. Pa-lo-wah-ti-wa wore a red eagle plume, the mark of his rank as chief warrior of the Little Fire Order. Na-na-he wore also a red plume and white eagle plume, indicating his rank in the Little Fire and Rattlesnake Orders, and for the same reason was painted with red about the eyes, with yellow of the Kâ-kâ beneath. After the arrangement of their paraphernalia they were faced to the east, and Nai-iu-tchi blew over them the sacred medicine-powder of the flowers (yellow pollen), designed not only to insure good feeling from the gods, but also to make the hearts of all strangers present happy toward themselves.

Each member took in his left hand the plume-sticks of his order, while the 'plumes of special sacrifice to the deities of the ocean, as well as the sacred-cane cigarettes prepared and consecrated in Zuñi by the Priest of the Sun, were placed in a sacred basket brought for the purpose. Nai-iu-tchi, who headed the party, carried the ancient net-covered and fringed gourd which had held the water for centuries and was the vessel to be first filled; Lai-iu-ah-tsai-lun-k'ia followed with the basket and two vases of spar; Ki-ä-si and Mr. Cushing came next, each with one of the sacred it "whizzers" without which no solemn ceremonial would be complete in the presence of the gods. Last came Pa-lo-wah-ti-wa and Na-na-he. Proceeding at once to the beach, Nai-iu-tchi silently directed the rest to a stony point off to the left, which he deemed preferable to the sandy shore for two reasons: because it entered farther east into the ocean, and because stony points and wild places are considered more frequented by the animal gods, and more acceptable places for the sacrifice of plumes. Sacred meal was there scattered about to form the consecrated bed of the ceremonials, and all squatted in regular order, facing the east and the open sea. Each member grasped in both hands his plumes and began moving them up and down as though to keep time with the song which followed, which was low, plaintive, and filled with expressions of praise and entreaty to the gods of the ocean. At four intervals during the singing of each stanza sacred meal was scattered out over the waves. This song-prayer, or chant, was, like most music of the Zuñis, in perfect unison. With every in coming wave the tide rose higher and higher, soon covering their feet, and at last the rocks upon which they were sitting. Being ignorant of the tidal laws, they recognized in the tide the coming of the beloved gods of the ocean to greet them in token of pleasure at their work. As Mr. Cushing shrank back, they said: "Little brother, be prepared and firm; why should you fear our beloved mother?—for that it should be thus we came over the road unto the land of sunrise. What though the waves swallow us up? They would embrace us, not in anger, but in gratitude for our trust, and who would hesitate to have his light of life cut off by the beloved?" At the close of their song, and urged by Mr. Cushing, the Indians reluctantly moved back to the sandy beach. Here a double row was formed not far from the water, the sacred cigarettes were lit by the two high priests, and after puffs to the six points

BURYING THE SACRED PLUME-STICKS IN THE OCEAN.

of the universe—North, West, South, East, and the upper and lower regions—they were handed around. After the saying of a prayer by each, according to rank in the religious orders, the plumed prayer-sticks were invested with the influence of prayer by breathing smoke from the cigarette deeply into the lungs, and then blowing it out among the feathers. These were then taken up, and cast upon the waters. The vessels were then grasped by Nai-iu-tchi and Lai-iu-ah-tsai-lun-k'ia, who, with bared legs and feet, waded into the sea and poured upon its surface the "meal of all foods," brought for the purpose from Zuñi. Then, first sprinkling water to the six regions and upon the assembled multitude, they dipped the sacred vessels full, and, while they were standing knee-deep engaged in prayer, Ki-a-si and Mr. Cushing advanced, dipping the points of their whizzers into the water, and followed them in prayer. The two priests started up out of the water, and the latter began, the one to the left and the other to the right, to whirl their whizzers, and followed the four others toward the tent. Inside, they formed in a row and sang a song celebrating the acquisition of the waters—a strange chant, which, from its regularity and form, Mr. Cushing considered traditional, yet which he had never before heard of. At the close of each stanza was the refrain:

"Over the road to the middle of the world [Zuñi] thou willst go!"

On each repetition of this their hands were stretched far out toward the west, and sacred meal was scattered still farther in that direction. A prayer in which consideration was asked for the children of the Zuñis, of the Americans, and of all men, of the beasts and birds of the world, and of even the creeping and most vile beings of earth, and the most insignificant, concluded the ceremonial. The Indians then seized the seven demijohns given them by the city, which, with their patent wooden covering, looked like models of grain-elevators, and took them down to the beach, where they filled them without farther ceremony.

Before their return to the city a rite unexpected to Mr. Cushing followed, being the first step toward his initiation into the Kâ-kâ, It consisted of baptism with water taken from the sea, and embraces, with prayers. It was the ceremonial of adoption before the gods and in the presence of the spirits, preliminary to introduction into any of the orders of the Zuñis.

Sylvester Baxter.

NATIONAL SEAL OF THE ZUÑIS.

THE FATHER OF THE PUEBLOS

AROUND THE COUNCIL FIRE.

High upon the western slope of the Sierra Madre, in New Mexico, nearly a mile and a half above the sea-level, and but a few miles beyond the divide, where scanty waters begin their timid and uncertain way down toward the Pacific, stands ancient Zuñi, the father of the pueblos. When Coronado made his famous march into the unknown North, the Zuñis, or Shi-wi-nas, as they call themselves, were the first, and also the most numerous and powerful, of the pueblo people encountered by him. Their towns covered a great territory, almost deserving the name of "kingdom" —term so lavishly and loosely used by Coronado and his contemporary explorers. Oppression and pestilence have so diminished their numbers, and their strict exclusiveness has so impoverished their physical condition, that the once mighty nation has now been reduced to a handful of people. These inhabit a single pueblo. But the country around is dotted with ruined towns upon whose walls is graven the symbol of the shi-wi-na, the sacred water-spider, whose figure forms the Zuñi coat of arms. Here, surrounded by the forsaken homes of their kindred and ancestry—crumbling heaps which in antiquity rival the storied stones of the Old World—the Zuñis live as their fathers lived, and jealously treasure their proud history.

Zuñi is still the largest of the pueblos of New Mexico and Arizona, and is looked up to by the others, which differ entirely in language, with the veneration and homage belonging to the elder member of their family, the source whence come their religion and institutions. By the census of 1880, under an accurate count, the population of Zuñi numbered 1602, nearly 500 more than that of Isleta, the next pueblo in size. Therefore it is still a considerable town. It is only a few years since the Zuñis numbered several thousand, but an epidemic of the small-pox decimated them terribly.

With the exception of the Moquis and the Java Supais, or Ku'h-nis, in Arizona—the latter an almost unknown pueblo in Cataract Creek Cañon, one of the "box cañons" of the Colorado—the Zuñis, are the most isolated of all the pueblo tribes. They have therefore been little influenced by contact either with Spanish or Anglo-American civilization, and to-day live substantially the life they led when Coronado first started out in search of the seven cities of Cibola. The river pueblos, as they are called—those ranging along the Rio Grande from Taos to Isleta—have monopolized the attention of travellers and writers, being the most convenient of access. But these, surrounded by the towns of the Mexicans on every hand, and latterly having come in contact with the more pushing American, who leaves his own indelible impress upon all whom he meets, they have naturally been materially influenced by the alien life around them, and their manners have been considerably changed thereby.

However good a copy may be, however faithful as a reproduction, the most of us have a strong preference for originals. So Zuñi, as the oldest of the pueblo families, as the father of their *Kultur*, as the Germans would say, and possessing the most distinctive characteristics, is decidedly the representative pueblo of New Mexico. For this reason, and because it had been little touched even by the pioneer tourists who have been brought to the new Southwest by the advent of railroads, we decided to visit it. It was well that we do so, for a mind of rare scientific attainments had been attracted thither for similar reasons, and the company of its possessor proved of much profit and pleasure to us.

The building of the new Atlantic and Pacific Railroad, with its strong, smooth track designed for heavy transcontinental travel, had just brought Zuñi within an easy day's wagon journey of one of the world's great highways, being about thirty miles southward from the military post of Fort Wingate, thus saving a fatiguing trip of many days across a forbidding country.

The land inhabited by the declining nation living on in the twilight of its ancient glory—worn out but not despondent, and lifting its head proudly to receive whatever fate may yet have to bestow before its life-sands run entirely out—the land also looks old and worn and weary of its prolonged battle of myriad centuries against the united elements: perhaps a foreshadowing of the time when the vital forces of all the globe shall be as spent as in this corner of it, and the great earthball swing its way through space as cold and dead and nakedly desolate as the lifeless, airless moon.

The hoary ruins of the other continent, draped with verdure of vines, and empowered and crowned with arborescent beauty, impress us with the age of mankind. But here the ruined earth itself, sprinkled with the ruined dwellings of man, tells with awful eloquence of the antiquity of both the world and its dominant animal. And it tells that the youth of both is so unspeakably far away in the past! Since the ocean rolled over the land and forsook it, and mighty rivers coursed their way across it, the forces of nature have cut far down into the earth's surface, have eaten into it, hewn it away, worn it down, and skimmed it off, until now the former level only remains in gigantic detached tables, standing mountain-like thousands of feet above the arid plains of to-day. And upon the old upper plain of these semsas the ocean has left its shells, and the prehistoric rivers their boulders and pebbles, their beds still left of the structure of a continent before its geography was remodelled.

As if in sublime mockery of the insignificance of man and his works, time has wrought these ruins of a remote geological era into curious and fantastic semblances of human ruins. The most wonderful and majestically beautiful of architectural forms are here, carved in the rich sandstone which ranges through all the warm hues from brown to red and yellow with gray and black for sober relief. Castles, halls, temples, with grand gables, terraces gateways, and porches, turrets and pinnacles, lofty towers and graceful spires, form vast Titanic cities. Though only the theatre of the dusk of a race of man, here well might be the scene of the *Götterdämmerung*.

And here the earth's ruins only are foliage-garbed and tree-crowned. Nature has kept her funeral wreaths for her own remains alone. Forests deck the roofs of this natural architecture, and their fringes drape the sides, flank the towers, adorn the buttresses, and fill the crevices of the magnificent masonry. These forests are mementos of the time when the life-giving ocean winds swept free across the young continent, and wove a green garment for all its surface. The same winds still touch what is left of their old haunts, and their breath has still the same magic power. But before they sink into the dry depths of the later plains their moisture is wrung away. Meanwhile the ruins of the man's buildings crouch pitiably bare at the feet of the mighty structures, with no leaves to cover their nakedness, as if Nature denied her consolation to man, the desecrater of the forest temples she reared for his protection—man, who by his sacrilege is covering the world's fairest fields with desolation, and hastening the day of the planet's death. May there not be prophecy in the Northern myth that when Iduna with her youth-giving apples is gone, leaving the gods gray and weak in the twilight of their power, then on the last day shall come Surtur from his realm of Muspelheim—the flame-world—and destroy the gods and the earth with his fiery sword? For the gods are but the powers of nature, and last day is Surtur's day.

At Fort Wingate—whose clustered buildings of light gray adobe look cheerfully out from a mountain-side background of dart green piños across a brown plain to a panorama of this architectural sublimity—while sitting in the officers' club room one warm afternoon, we saw a striking figure walking across the parade ground: a slender young man in a picturesque costume; a high-crowned and broad-brimmed felt hat above long blonde hair and prominent features; face, figure, and general aspect looked as if he might have stepped out of the frame of a cavalier's portrait of the time of King Charles. The costume, too,

FRANK H. CUSHING.

seemed at first glance to belong to the age of chivalry, though the materials were evidently of the frontier. There were knee-breeches, stockings, belt, etc., all of a fashion that would not have an unfamiliar look if given out as a European costume of two or three centuries ago. But it was a purely aboriginal dress, such as had been worn on that ground for ages.

Answering our inquiry, the army officer with whom we were talking said: "That is Frank H. Cushing, a young gentleman commissioned by the Smithsonian Institution to investigate the history of the pueblo Indians as it may be traced in their present life and customs. He is living at Zuñi, that being the best field for his researches. It is no streak of eccentricity that prompts him to dress that way; no desire to make himself conspicuous. He is one of the most modest fellows I ever knew, and the attention attracted by such a costume is really painful to him. But he bears it without flinching, as bravely as he has borne many perils and privations in the cause of science. He has an end in view, and wisely adopts the means best suited to its attainment. That is the course taken by all men successful in whatever may be their chosen pursuits. Stanley would have been a fool to wear the fur clothing of the artic regions, or even his native starched linen, on his expedition into the heart of Africa. Neither would a miller follow his trade in a suit of black broadcloth. So Cushing, to make a success of his investigations, can not stand contemplating his subjects from the outside, like a spectator at a play. He must go on to the stage, and take his own part in the performance. There are no people more distrustful of the motives of strangers than are the North American Indians. One can only learn anything trustworthy from them by gaining their confidence and sympathy; so Cushing has adopted the only sensible course. He has become one of the Zuñis for the time being, has conformed to all their observances, and learned their language thoroughly. He has been made their second chief, and is a recognized leader among them. His reward is that the curtain of a mysteriously hidden past and present has been lifted for him. To a primitive people rank and authority are most powerfully indicated by their outward symbols. To maintain his influence, Cushing must out-Zuñi the Zuñis, so to speak. A man sent to them from the great father at Washington, and with means and leisure, as he seems to have, must dress according to his station. And it pleases and flatters them to see him always arrayed in the full traditional costume of their nation—a dress such as they only wear on formal occasions. He is amply rewarded for all such conformities to their pleasure. As you are intending a trip to Zuñi, gentlemen, you ought by all means to meet him. To be there with him will alone make it worth your while to have come across the continent. His companionship will give you an insight into the life of a strange people whose strangeness is passing quickly away—a life which otherwise you could hope to know only by what the uninstructed, and therefore deceiving, vision might tell you."

We soon met Mr. Cushing, and spent a few pleasant days with him at the fort. The knowledge gained by our intercourse, which developed a warm mutual friendship, proved to be the finest preparation for the trip, like "reading up" before setting out on a tour to strange countries. Mr. Cushing was visiting his friend Dr. Washington Matthews, the post surgeon, and was engaged in packing some rare specimens to go to the Smithosonian Institution. Dr. Matthews was in hearty sympathy with Mr Cushing's work, being himself an able ethnologist, who has made a reputation by his researches among the Hidatzas of the Northern plains, and is now making similar studies among the Navajos. Another energetic worker in the aboriginal field, whose duty happened to call him to Fort Wingate at the time, was Lieutenant Bourke, of General Crooke's staff, detailed to make special studies of the habits of the Indians. Lieutenant Bourke was modestly depreciatory of the value of his own work in comparison with that of Mr. Cushing, whom he termed the ablest American ethnologist. But Lieutenant Bourke's investigations, as recorded in his accurate and remarkably full notes, can not fail to form valuable contributions to ethnological science.

It was an early June morning, with hot sunshine, but clear, invigorating air, when we started in a four-mule ambulance on our trip of thirty miles to Zuñi. There were four of us—Mr. Cushing, a young lieutenant, the artist, and the writer. We were soon high up on the wooded uplands of the Zuñi range, enjoying on the ascent backward views over great plains expanding away to the blue distance of Arizona mountains. The forest scenery of the mountain heights was in delightful contrast to the dusty plain's dry waste. The road wound through shady groves of tall and sturdy pines, their trunks marked with clean red bark; also cedars with bark in queer gray scales, like the back of an alligator, The woods stood, not with closed ranks like an Eastern forest, but open and part-like, interspersed with beautiful grassy glades: just the places for grazing deer.

Time sped quickly in listening to Mr. Cushing's willing replies to our multitudinous inquiries. "If you are told that any primitive people is ignorant of its history, don't believe it," said he. "They know all about it." And he told with what wonderful accuracy traditions are handed down among the Zuñis, the tales, repeated thousands of times, being transmitted from father to son without the change of a single word, for generation after generation. Reliance on written words seems to impair the retentive power of the memory of lettered races, and the marvellous memorizing capacity of illiterate peoples is illustrated in the handing down of the grand old Northern sagas by the Icelanders, until the acquisition of the alphabet enabled them to be recorded by the great author Snorri Sturluson; also the transmission for generations, among the same people, of the most intricate of genealogical details, involving the history of widely branched families for centuries, and covering all the lands of Scandinavia.

In the same way the Zuñis have an extensive unwritten literature, if the expression may be permitted. They have a vast accumulation of fables and folk-lore, and the past of the nation is given in what may be termed the Zuñi Bible. This sacred work is publicly recited at rare but regularly recurring intervals. It is in four divisions corresponding to four chapters. Its recitation occupies two long evenings. It is in perfect rhyme and rhythm, and is highly poetic. When Mr. Cushing first came to Zuñi the charge of the Bible was officially intrusted to an aged, white-haired, and blind old man, a veritable native Homer. This was the sole duty of the bard, and he was supported by the public. He died, and the succession came to one of four whom he had trained up. These four are in turn continually instructing youth qualified of the high trust by birth and lineage.

To acquire and record this wonderful work, the Zuñi Bible, would be a Homeric task. Mr. Cushing has several times had the privilege of listening to its recital—it is very often recited informally; but to memorize it and write it down would demand the closest application. To get it repeated often enough for such a purpose would need the use of the nicest diplomacy. The Bible begins with the mythical origin of the people, and then enters upon what is evidently genuine history. This is brought down to comparatively recent times, but the work ends before the era of the Spanish conquest is reached. The story of the Zuñis is told from the time when their home was on the shore of the great ocean to the westward, probably in Southern California, and the various changes of abode are given during their migration to their present seat in the land of Cibola, as the country of the Zuñis, after much historical controversy, is now fully proven to be by Mr. Cushing. The sites of the seven cities of Cibola, described by Coronado and Friar Niza, have been accurately fixed by Mr. Cushing; they are in the immediate neighborhood of the present pueblo of Zuñi, which was established upon its present site not long after the Spanish conquest, having been removed from its location near by.

The accuracy of the information possessed by Zuñis concerning the ruined towns where their ancestry lived is marvellous. These towns were successively settled and abandoned for various causes, chief among which were the pressure of the hostile people, and the choking with sand of the springs upon which they depended. The history of these places, which are almost innumerable, is mostly back in obscure antiquity, as is certified by time's imprint upon the ruins. The region in which these ruins are found covers a large part of New Mexico and Arizona. Every investigation of ruins claimed by the Zuñis as theirs—their locations often having been unknown until Mr. Cushing was told that the Zuñis once lived in certain places, to be distinguished by certain marks and features—has verified their statements, their accuracy always proving unerring.

The language of the Zuñis is the reverse of barbarically crude, as might perhaps be expected of an aboriginal tongue. It has a finely ordered structure, and is very expressive, abounding in delicate shadings, and allowing fine distinctions of meaning. The order of sentences resembles that of Latin and German rather than English. The Zuñis are fastidious in their requirements for the correct use of the language, and are intolerant of ungrammatical speech; and, strange to say, they have an ancient or classical language, spoken centuries ago, handed down in the many sacred songs, and used to-day in their religious observances. This dead language bears a similar relation to their speech of to-day as Anglo-Saxon to English. It is not understood by the common people, but is familiar only to the priests and leading men. So here too is the Church the conservator of ancient erudition.

On every hand are met startling resemblances to the familiar civilizations of the East. The folk-lore, the recital of whose tales and fables begins after the frost comes, and fills the long winter evenings at the family firesides, offers many of these parallels. Some of their fables are, in substance, almost identical with fables of Æsop. For spells and incantations the Zuñis use short rhymed couplets, just as did our Saxon ancestors. Their religious ceremonials are strangely like those of the ancient Egyptians and Greeks. A striking analogy between the Zuñi and the Northern mythology is found in the characterization of the spirit of evil. The Zuñis have two names for the Evil One, meaning respectively "the maliciously bad" and the "stupidly bad." In the same way the Northern mythology has two evil spirits—Loki, the cunning demon, the spirit of intelligent wickedness, who often dresses evil in an alluring guise, and the strong but blind Hödur, in whom the evil coming from the possession of power by ignorance is typified, Hödur killing unwittingly his beautiful brother Baldur with the lance of mistletoe placed in his hand by the sly Loki. In view of these many resemblances, the query has been raised if the story of the lost Atlantis, the sunken continent, might not be something more than a myth. Might not this, the older continent, be the ancestral home of the oldest races of the Eastern world? Or do these resemblances simply show that for the mental development of man there are certain set forms, that these repeat themselves everywhere, and that the human intellect passes through regular stages of progression, of which these similarities are marks? These are questions which ethnology may be able to answer some day when it has become a more positive science.

Meanwhile we had begun to ascent the southerly slope of the Zuñi range, and the steepness of the way, together with its roughness, was calculated to arouse serious misgivings about arriving safely at the bottom. For a new sensation, driving on the plains and among the mountains of the Southwest may be commended. A team will fearlessly plunge, with brakes firmly set, down the banks of a deep arroyo—the dry bed of a torrent—and jauntily storm the almost perpendicular opposite bank. In an Eastern town the existence of such a road would fill the sleep of the selectmen with fearful nightmares of suits for damages to be brought by the owners of injured vehicles.

The beautiful valley of Las Nutrias (The Beavers) now lay smiling before us with fertile fields of growing crops, and ringed around by ruggedly picturesque mountains, sharp rocks and sombre pines contrasting with the peaceful beauty of the scene below. Las Nutrias is one of three or four small pueblos which, since the reduction of the tribe, have in recent years been abandoned as permanent abiding-places, but are used as summer residences, where people live while they tend their fields. The entire population is now concentrated at Zuñi.

Crossing a brook whose waters irrigated the broad fields around, we halted at one of these "summer villas" to rest for lunch. Its structure was rather different from the regular dwellings we afterward became familiar with. Like them, its walls were solidly built of adobe and stone, but in front was a sort of veranda, and a wide space had been cut away in the wall of the principal room, a large apartment, which was thus made into a sort of airy, open hall. The noonday was hot outside, but within there was an agreeable coolness, the light, dry air of these altitudes not retaining the heat away from the sunshine. An old man and a white-haired wife welcomed us cordially, and chatted vivaciously with "Kuishy," as they called our friend, while a chubby brown boy of four or five years, with pretty face and black mischievous eyes, romped around us. To the lunch we had brought along, the old woman added by setting before us a basket of parched corn, which proved something like our parched sweet corn. They always slightly parch their corn before grinding it into meal, spreading it out in the dome-shaped ovens which stand outside their doors, and often on their roofs, forming, as in the Orient, prominent architectural features of their dwellings.

Lunch over, we set out again, but a sick mule made our progress tediously slow. Under the circumstances, finding that it would be impossible to reach Zuñi that night, we turned toward Pescado, another of the summer suburbs, named for a fine large spring near by, full of little fish. This spring gushes out beautifully from beneath a lava rock, giving fertility to a large district. Though eating many strange things, as we soon had opportunity to see, the Zuñis, together with other Southwestern Indians, have their own ideas of fastidiousness; and one thing which neither they nor the Navajos will touch is fish, showing the most intense disgust at the idea of eating it. Therefore the finny inhabitants which give their name to the Pescado spring remain undiminished in number.

The Governor of Zuñi, whom we had already met at the fort a few days before, was a Pescado attending to his farm. He was at work in a field near the road as we approached, and came to meet us. A joyful gleam illuminated his dusky face as he recognized "his young brother," and as he walked along beside our slowly moving team he humorously responded to Kuishy's playful queries. A member of the most powerful family of Zuñi, Petricio Piño is a man of middle age, with a thoughtful, reflective face, and a profile that is almost classically Greek. We reached Pescado none too soon, for the moment we stopped, our sick mule fell to the ground, and in a few minutes was dead.

The cloudless sunset was speedily followed by calm moonlight and the night air had begun to have a touch of chilliness in it when we were summoned in to supper—climbing up a ladder, and entering through the roof of a house that probably antedated the Spanish conquest, for Pescado is much older than the present Zuñi. A large L-shaped room, with a low ceiling, and dingy walls hung with blankets and weapons, was lit by the flickering flame in a corner fire-place, where a large kettle was steaming and sending out an odor of stewing meat grateful to the nostrils of hungry men. Two large bowls of the smoking stew were dished out; one was set before us, and we drew around it, sitting on sheep-skins and blankets spread over the earthen floor, while the dusky members of the household formed a circle around the other, close by. The dish was really excellent, a kind of thick mutton broth, with whole grains of wheat to give it body, and agreeably flavored with a kind of herb highly prized by the Zuñis. Rolls of the peculiar "paper bread" were given to us. In eating it, it is the custom to dip the end of the roll into the broth. The liquid part was eaten with a sort of spoon made of pottery—a spoon without a handle, but at the upper end of the bowl, where the handle should be, it was curved over backward so that could be hung on the edge of the dish. There were, of course, no knives and forks, and the meat was taken out with the fingers. We learned that we had quite won the hearts of our hosts by doing in Rome as the Romans did; for they had been accustomed to see white visitors manifest much squeamishness about their food, and not unfrequently gingerly refuse to touch it at all.

As an "entrée," a dish of roasted locusts was handed around. The writer did not venture to try them, but his companions did. They are said to be as delicate and delicious as shrimps, with a similar flavor. Mur Cushing confessed that, although he made it a rule to everything that the Zuñis did, he never could get over a certain repugnance to the idea of eating these locusts. But as lobsters, crabs, and shrimps are insects as well as locusts, there seems to be no logical reason why the latter should not be as edible as the others. To catch them, the holes where the locust larvæ lie are watched in the early morning. Just as the first rays of the sun strike the ground, they all appear simultaneously, as if at a signal call. The ground is suddenly covered with them, and they are captured by thousands, and taken home in baskets and bowls. They are put to soak in cold water, and left to stand overnight. This fattens them, and in the morning they are roasted in a dish over the fire, the mass being continually stirred until of a nice uniform brown.

After supper we lay back upon the sheepskins, quietly enjoying the novel scene about us. Sticks of pin wood had been placed on end in the corner of the fireplace, and their bright crackling flame sent a ruddy light through the large room, touching up the nearer side of all objects in sharp relief against the intensity of the shadows. Gay-colored clothing and blankets, hung on poles suspended from the ceiling, caught the dancing light; curious pottery was ranged along the floor by the walls; and here and there in the walls were little niches, just as we had seen them in the walls of ruined cliff dwellings. In these little niches were conveniently arranged little articles of domestic use, which had a delightfully bric-à-brac suggestiveness. The scene was just the same now as it had been within those walls hundreds of years before. We were away back in the centuries, and living the life of the remote past.

We started late the next morning. In the distance, here and there among the mountains, thin blue smoke curled up in the calm air. It came from fires which the Zuñis had made to burn over the ground for planting their peach orchards in favorably situated cañons, where the trees would be sheltered from the blasting winds. In these places the Zuñis raise an abundance of peaches of a delicious quality.

We passed along the base of a mesa whose steep sandstone sides were fantastically worn. In one projecting angle there was a large opening in the rock, through which the sky on the other side could plainly be seen. The Goddess of Salt, say the Zuñis in one of their myths, was so troubled by the people who lived around her home on the shores of the great ocean that she forsook them, and came to live in this region, where she wedded the God of Turquoise. They lived happily together for a long time; but at last the people here also became troublesome to her, and she left them, and disappeared in this mountain, making this hole by her entrance. But in passing through, one of her plumes was brushed off, and it remains to this day in the shape of the high monument of stone standing in the plain close by. The resting-places of the goddess are marked by the salt lakes, including the large one to the south of Zuñi-land, from which the Zuñis gather their salt. In recognition of the ownership of the Zuñis in this lake, other Indian tribes who get salt there have always paid them toll for the privilege, and the lake has thus been a considerable source of revenue for them. The favor of the goddess for the Zuñis was markedly shown in this bequest. The footsteps of the God of Turquoise are marked by the turquoise deposits in the mountains.

PORTAL AND PLUME OF THE GODDESS OF SALT.

We reached Zuñi at noon. The pueblo lies near the foot of the majestic mesa of Tá-ai-iä-lo-ne—the sacred thunder mountain. Close to the town flows the Zuñi River. Whoever knows the stream will smile broadly at the instructions give a government exploring expedition sent out soon after the annexation of New Mexico. The commander was charged expressly to examine the Colorado, Chiquito, and the Zuñi rivers, with particular reference to their value for steamboat navigation. The stream is generally so shallow that in most places its waters would hardly reach above the ankles, and for considerable stretches in its course it loses itself in the sand altogether. But in the wet season the river often becomes a powerful torrent; it was for this reason that the pueblo, which once stood on the left bank, where it was subject to inundations, was, not long after the conquest, removed to its present site on the right bank, which is somewhat bluff-like at this place. The knoll upon which Zuñi stands seems higher than it really is, owing to the way in which the houses are terraced above each other, giving the place a commanding appearance as it is approached. The prevailing tone of the pueblo and the surrounding landscape is red. Such is the hue of grand old Tá-ai-iä-lo-ne's face; the pueblo is build chiefly of red sandstone largely excavated from the ruins of the elder Zuñi across the river, the thin slabs, about the thickness of ancient Roman bricks, being laid in red adobe mortar from the tawny soil; and the wide stretching plain around is red, and worn bare of all vegetation by the thousands of sheep owned in Zuñi, and kept in the corrals, made of scrawny upright sticks, surrounding the place like a girdle of thorns.

Mr. Cushing's room at the house of the Governor was a picturesque mingling of culture and barbarism. A writing-table, a case of book-shelves with the books necessary to his studies, and the volumes of valuable notes that recorded his investigations, a stool, a student-lamp, and a hammock, completed the inventory of the civilized furnishings. But there was the addition of a telephone which Mr. Cushing and his brother, who was visiting him, constructed out of a couple of old tin cans and several hundred yards of twine, to prove to the Zuñis the truth of what he had told them about the triumphs of American invention. The telephone was connected with the house of one of the caciques on the opposite side of the pueblo, about a quarter of a mile away. The Zuñis found it the most marvellous thing they had ever seen, and an old fogy among them, who had scoffed at it as beyond reason, on satisfying himself of its reality, stood beside it all day when it was first tested, watching its operation with intense interest. The hard earthen floor of the room was covered with Navajo and Pueblo blankets, their bright hues making them admirable for rugs—a purpose for which they are used with artistic effect in the quarters of the officers at various military posts in New Mexico. The walls were also hung with some choice examples of the blankets, giving a novel tapestry effect. With the photographs of some home friends adorning the wall, the room had a charmingly bright and cozy look.

Against the outside wall of the house were built large cages for the eagles, which are kept for the sake of their highly valued plumes. Eagle-farming is carried on among the Zuñis to a considerable extent. The majestic birds had lately been plucked, giving them a comically disreputable look, by no means in concert with the piercing, fearless gaze of their bright eyes. They were by no means tame, and even the tormenting spirit of the Zuñi children could not tempt those imps of mischief to transgress the bounds of a respectful distance from the cages. A blow from those powerful beaks would leave a mark never to be forgotten. The dignity of these eagles was unruffled—something that could hardly be said of their plumage just then—and a slight turn of the head was all the notice their majesties condescended to take of by-standers.

The Zuñi children sported around the streets in cherubic nakedness. They were as rompingly mischievous as any children can be, and their delight in torment seemed abnormally developed, perhaps because their elders saw nothing out of the way in it. Most likely the savage love to torture in warfare may be ascribed to this. The poor dogs fared hard at the children's hands. Not unfrequently during our visit a succession of piercing yelps would be heard, while a poor cur disappeared rapidly around the corner, fleeing from a terrorizing piece of ancient pottery tied to his ruined tail, while a crowd of urchings yelling with delight followed at his heels. And the unhappy hogs straggling around in the outskirts, which nobody seemed to feel a proprietary interest in—no wonder that they were gaunt and razor-backed and never grew fat! No wonder that the Zuñis had no appreciation of the delicacy of pork! The wretched grunters were chased and hectored by the children from morn to night, until they became too exhausted to resist, and would submit listlessly to the wills of their tormentors. With such sharp, bristle-covered backs as characterized these swine, it was a marvel how the naked brats could take such pleasure in riding them.

It was a prettier sight to see the chubby brown bodies of the children as they lay by the dozen dabbling in the tepid waters of the river all through the hot hours, soaking in the pools, or scampering along the alkali-incrusted banks, nosily splashing each other. One thing to be said to their credit is that in their disagreements they never came to blows. The admirable Indian trait of considering it beneath the dignity of a human being to strike another seems to be inherent. The children are tenderly loved by their parents, and their training is carefully looked after. They have the universal child-love of toys, and the little girls cherish maternally rude woollen dolls. A favorite toy for the babies is a little stuffed kid.

Outside the line of the corrals for the ponies, sheep, and goats were the queer little gardens of the women. They were divided into small rectangular lots, separated by stake fences and often by substantial walls of adobe, with narrow alleyways running between them. These little gardens looked for all the world like collections of gigantic waffles, being divided into rectangular beds, each bed cut up by intersecting ridges of earth. The little spaces thus formed appeared to be of almost mathematical exactness in size, and were planted with onions and herbs. These little squares were thus ridged about to hold the water with which the ground was kept moist, each square receiving the contents of a large water jar. The gardens were carefully tended by the women, and looked wonderfully neat. All around on the plain were the corn fields, where crops were raised without irrigation, a remarkable thing for such a dry climate. The corn was planted very deep in holes punched with a sharp stick, and was very low in growth, the ears branching out from the stalk close to the ground. Maize had been raised in this way for ages. There are no irrigating ditches about Zuñi itself, but at Pescado, Las Nutrias, and Ojo Caliente the crops are elaborately irrigated. The labor in the

TÁ-AI-IÄ-LO-NE, OR THUNDER MOUNTAIN.

fields is done by the men, who in all the pueblo tribes do not consider, as the savage Indians do, manual labor as something fit only for squaws.

The street scenes of Zuñi seem thoroughly Oriental. Narrow winding ways and irregular-shaped plazas, all of which have characteristic names, give the town a quaint picturesqueness. In places the terraced building tower to a height worthy of metropolitan structures. Low passageways carry the thoroughfare under the buildings here and there, giving artistic contrasts of light and shade, while the oddly costumed figures in the streets make a striking picture. The monotony of blank walls is here and there broken by the rude but massive stairways leading to second stories, rows of round projecting roof beams, and the giant ladders leaning against the buildings everywhere, each stretching two thin arms skyward. All the inhabitants have a sailor-like agility in the use of the ladders. The women go up and down with water jars on their heads without touching a hand to support or steady themselves; little children, hardly out of babyhood, scramble fearlessly up and down; even the dogs have a squirrel-like nimbleness, trotting in a matter-of-course way down the rounds of a steep ladder. If there were any more trees in Zuñi than the solitary cottonwood standing in the yard before the ruined Franciscan chapel, it would hardly be surprising to see the dogs climbing them like cats!

All through the day there is an unceasing carrying of water, the women passing and repassing through the streets on the way to and from the springs with the large ollas, or water jars, so nicely balanced on their heads as not to spill a drop, and walking with a fine, erect poise. But toward sunset is the time to visit the great spring on the hill-side just outside the city. It is a Scripture-like scene. Descending by a path between steep banks of clay, we come upon a large pool in an excavated cavern, a round chamber in the hill-side, and entered by a great arch-like opening. Here in the cool shadow crowds of girls come and go, dipping up the water, and pausing to gossip as they meet in the path or beside the well. Their soft voices fill the air like the chatter of swallows, and their white teeth gleam as they laugh. As they come down the sloping path the slanting sunlight touches up the bits of bright color that adorn their dark costumes, and their figures are bathed in a mellow glow, while those further down between the high banks are dusky in the gathering shadows.

Wandering through the place, we enter, according to the custom of the natives, any of the open doorways at pleasure, stroll quietly about the house, examine the pottery, blankets, and other household goods, the family meanwhile looking on with courteous curiosity. "I-mu" (be seated), they say; and if they are at their meals, one is welcome to join them, even though it chance to be their last crust. The woman of the house is perhaps at work baking paper bread. She takes a fresh sheet just off the fire, and making a roll of it, hands it over to us. In her work she sits by the fire-place with a dish of the pasty corn-meal dough beside her made rather thin. She has no superfluous raiment, for the fire is hot. With a quick motion she takes a handful and skillfully spreads it over a large smooth stone slab, underneath which the fire is burning. It is baked almost immediately, being spread so thin. As soon as done, the sheets are laid above each other, until they form a considerable pile. They are in various colors, yellow, blue, green, or red, according to the color of the corn, which is carefully sorted, when shelled, with a view to this effect.

In their way the Zuñis are paragons of politeness, and the most polished nation of Europe could hardly excel them in genuine courtesy. One of them after shaking hands—they are great for hand-shaking—may be seen to lift his hand to his lips and reverently breathe upon it, an action designed to breathe into himself whatever superior influence from the other person may have been received by the friendly contact. Here is a dialogue between two Zuñis about to smoke. Says one:

"Why do you not light your cigarette!"

"Are you older than I?" asks the other.

"Yes."

"Then light yours first, for whoever goes before his elder brother will surely stumble."

The Zuñi houses have large rooms and real doors, contrasting agreeably with the close little cells of many of the pueblos in the region near Santa Fe, which are entered only through the roof. It is not uncommon to see a large room with three or four fire-places, each of a different pattern, one designed, for roasting meat, another for baking bread, another for boiling, etc. These fire-places have a quaint mediæval look. They are generally built in the corner, with a large square hood flaring out over them from the chimney. A double fire-place may be built against the centre of a long side wall, and an immense broad fire-place often takes up the entire end of a room. A style consisting of a little arch in the corner is like those of Mexican houses; the other varieties are native, and are found in the oldest ruins.

The houses are owned by the women. The Zuñis are strictly monogamous, while savage Indian tribes are polygamous. This contrast between two branches of the same race, one living a settled and other a roving life, shows that monogamy is an essential condition of the former, and is an effective argument against one of the cardinal doctrines of Mormonism. The Zuñi women are by no means the slaves of the men. They have their rights, and maintain them. When a man marries, he goes to live with his wife, and if dissatisfied with him, she has the right to send him away. Therefore a husband is pretty careful to keep in his wife's good graces.

As one of the great annual dances was to come off, we waited a week for the sake of seeing it. Its regular time was at the full moon in May, but the two boys whose duty it was to repeat certain long prayers belonging to the ceremonials in the estufa had died, and novices had to be trained up in their places. Since the two prayers had to be committed word for word as they had been said for centuries, it was a long task, and the dance had to be postponed to the full moon of June.

Meanwhile the time passed quickly for us. During the day a mild hum of industry pervaded the place. The Zuñis take life easily, and never overwork, therefore they find no necessity for a periodic day of rest, but they are not lazy. Their wants are simple, and their work is ample to satisfy them. One of the most interesting things was to see them weave their fabrics on their hand-looms, producing beautiful designs by the nice calculation of the eye, but with no regular measurement. Our principal excitements during the week were the searching out of attractive blankets, either Navajo or Pueblo, and the opening of kilns of new pottery. Each family makes all its own pottery, as a usual thing, and every day kilns were burning all over the place. The news that a finely decorated *olla* had been seen going into a kiln in a certain street was enough to set us agog, watching to see it come out freshly burned. One household had a special reputation for making fine *ollas*, another for small ware, another for figures of animals, and one woman was famed for making very nice turtles. The vessels to be burned were arranged carefully on the ground, and a circular, dome-shaped structure of dried sheep's dung built up around and over them. This fuel is preserved carefully in hard-pressed, flat blocks, and is kept corded up for use. It gives an intense heat, and a kiln is baked in two or three hours.

Archæologists have been puzzled by the occasional discovery of fragments of hard pottery with glazed decorative lines, and theories have been formed that among the ancient Pueblos the art of glazing their pottery was known. But Mr. Cushing has discovered that this glazing is accidental, occurring only in the broken pieces of old pottery used to cover the articles in the kiln and protect them from the falling of structure when it has mostly burned away. These fragments are made harder by the second firing, which also glazes certain mineral pigments used in their decoration.

Another interesting industry was the grinding of meal or flour. A row of girls, sometimes half a dozen or so, is often seen at work. They all kneel beside and over a series of bins, each of which has a bottom of smooth stone hollowed in a semi-circular shape. Each girl holds a bar of stone in her hands, and grinds the corn by rubbing it up and down with a motion much like that of a washer-woman at a scrubbing board. The meal, ground course in one bin, is passed on to the next, where the stone bar is of a finer texture, and so on to the end, when it is often ground as fine as flour. The jet-black hair of the girls, cut off about half-way down their face, forms a short thick veil, which is tossed up and down by the violent motion, their eyes showing brightly through as they regard the strangers.

The artist's work was a source of wonder to the Zuñis, and they looked upon his spirited portrayals with intense interest. They were, until recently, extremely superstitious about portraits, and nothing would induce any of them to allow their pictures to be made. They believed that something of their actual personality went with their likeness, and that whoever possessed it would also possess a certain control over themselves—a control which might bring evil upon them. But Mr. Cushing, who has talent for sketching which has been of great service to him in his notes, banished this superstition. It nearly cost him his life one time. But they saw that no evil came of it, and so they outgrew their objections. There seems to be no Chinese conservatism about them, but when they see the light, they readily accept it. In Mr. Cushing's earlier days in Zuñi his sketching caused a secret resolve to be made to kill him for practices that might bring disaster them all. It was to be done at a great dance that was soon to come off. He sat upon a neighboring house-top with sketch-book in hand, when two hideous figures among the dancers, painted a diabolical black, came to the foot of the adjacent ladder and pounded upon it with their war-clubs, shouting out something which caused the multitude to look toward him. He thought it a jocular part of the performance, and smiled good-naturedly. But he understood enough of the language at the time to distinguish the cries among the crowd: "Kill him! Kill him!" It was part of the performance to kill a symbolical Navajo, the Navajos being the ancient enemies of the Zuñis. Mr. Cushing had no idea that he was cast for the part of that Navajo, and did not comprehend the real gravity of the situation until he heard the women echo the cries, "Yes, kill him! Kill him!" The people rose up and looked his way. The assemblage was silent with expectations. He glanced behind; there was a wall of dark figures frowning down upon him, half muffled in their blankets and standing as immovable as statues. The twin friends below made ready to come up the ladder. Mr. Cushing now saw that his life was really threatened. A thousand against one! Attempt at escape was hopeless. He thought his last moment had come, and in his heart was terribly frightened. But to give way to fear was useless, and something told him to face the danger coolly. So he leisurely laid down his sketch-book, placed a stone upon the leaves to keep them from blowing in the wind, produced a new hunting-knife which he had just brought back with him from Fort Wingate, where he had been on a trip—nobody knew he had it—and flourished it, at the same time breaking out into a loud, defiant laugh. The evident coolness of the act, his boldness in facing them, took his assailants aback; they paused, and uttered a word meaning, "a spiritual friend," that is, a friend possessing supernatural characteristics, making him more than a common earthly friend—qualities which would bring good to them as a people.

MAKING POTTERY.

"A spiritual friend—we must not kill a spiritual friend!" cried the two; "but we must kill a Navajo!" they shouted.

So out of the court they rushed in search of a Navajo. A few minutes, and a fearful yelping was heard. In they rushed, dragging a "Navajo," in the shape of a great yellow cur half paralyzed with fright. They stunned him with their clubs; before he was dead they had him disemboweled, and in their frenzy were ravenously eating the smoked vitals. Mr. Cushing looked on in gratitude that he was not just then in the place of that dog, playing the part of a Navajo. But the event turned out to be the most fortunate thing for him; it fixed him in the affections of the whole tribe, and from that day was to be dated his great influence in Zuñi.

The superstition about portraits now lingered only among some of the old women—those conservators of the ancient order of things with all people. At Pescado the artist had made a sketch of a pretty little girl. At Zuñi Mr. Cushing showed it to the child's grandmother, a white-haired old crone, who looked at it intently for a moment, then left the room, sobbing wildly, saying, "My poor little Lupolita! How could you be so cruel as to let such an evil come upon her!"

One day the artist painted the portrait of Mr. Cushing's father by adoption, Lai-ui-ai-tsai-lun-k'iä, the high priest, or medicine cacique, one of the "seven great chiefs of the Zuñi." He was the personification of gentleness, and looked the mystic that he was by virtue of his high office: the Zuñis are spiritists, and their religion is in many striking phases identical with modern spiritism. In his face, which in its strongly individual lines resembled Dante's, there was an indescribably kindly and lovable contemplative expression—a spiritual look like one who walked the earth with thoughts in another sphere. His affection for "Kuishy," his adopted son, was touchingly tender. One day when the lieutenant was admiring a handsome silver belt of native manufacture belonging to him, the old cacique said to Mr. Cushing, "Remember, my son, that whatever I have is also yours, to do with as you please."

And one night in the council, when Mr. Cushing was talking rather excitedly on a matter that caused him some vexation, the old man got up and walked away quietly. "Where are you going, my father?" Mr. Cushing asked.

"It grieves me to see my son show his anger," said the old man, gently.

While the artist was painting his portrait, he sat motionless for something like three hours. In this respect the Indians are ideal models. Old Pedro Pino, the Governor's father, who for many years was himself Governor, sat and watched the work of painting with the keenest interest, announcing his intention not to go away until the thing was finished. Old Pedro was gray and wrinkled, and must have been over eighty years of age. He was in his prime when the Americans took possession of New Mexico, and was Governor of Zuñi at this time. He was full of reminiscences of those days, and was never tired of telling the lieutenant about the officers he knew, especially about Major Kendrick, who, old Pedro was delighted to hear, was one of the lieutenant's instructors at West Point. Old Pedro had much of the garrulity of age, but his talk plainly showed the native eloquence which marked the days of his power, when he used it with the skill of a trained diplomat, keeping his nation absolute followers of his will. When the portrait was completed, he talked long and earnestly to the venerable cacique. He told him: "Though your body perish, nevertheless you shall continue to live on upon the earth. Your face will not be forgotten now; though your hair turn gray, it will never turn gray here. I know this to be so, for I have seen, in the quarters of the officers at the fort, the faces of their fathers, who have long since passed from the earth, but still were looking down upon their children from the walls."

The Zuñis delight in a council. These councils are frequently held, there being no specified intervals of time for their sessions. They are called whenever occasion arises, and all affairs of the nation are discussed and regulated by them. They are legislatures and courts in one, and furnish an extremely interesting picture of parliamentarism in its primitive form. When a council is deemed necessary, the Governor orders his herald to summon it. At sunset, when the air is quiet, the herald stands upon the highest house-top in Zuñi—a statuesque figure against the clear sky—and utters the call in a loud, measured, and resonant voice. The women all hear it, and the tidings quickly spread, so that in the evening there is sure to be a good attendance. The herald answers for the newspaper in Zuñi, for all proclamations and items of news deemed of general importance are announced in this way.

After dusk on the evening of the council dark figures with blankets wrapped about them—for the evening air is always cool—enter the Governor's house silently as shadows. A grave salutation and a grasp of the hand, and they seat themselves in the large room used for the councils. One evening about a hundred of the leading men were thus assembled, sitting on a sort of bench running along side of the room, or squatting on their haunches in a circle. On the floor, in the midst of the circle, the Governor had strewn a lot of corn husks, and a bag of fine-cut being set out, cigarettes were rolled, and a constant smoking was kept up. The air would have been thick enough had not the large fireplaces given such excellent ventilation. The women and the young men gathered respectfully around the doors and windows and listened. As the evening wore on, the room grew warm, and the men gradually shed their garments, until about half the assemblage sat with naked bodies of a ruddy bronze hue. As it grew late, some arose and glided silently out of the room. But it was an important matter they were talking about, and the most of them staid until it was settled at a small hour of the morning. The subject was discussed earnestly and gravely, no emotion being shown either in the face or in the manner of speaking, although some would occasionally betray their excitement in a trembling voice. It was a will case under discussion, and the Governor sat motionless and speechless, being the judge from whose decision there could be no appeal. Early in the evening the two caciques who were present arose to go. In response to Mr. Cushing's question, Lai-ui-ai-tsai-lun-k'ia said, "Though it is our place to elect your Governor, it is not for us to say anything that may influence his judgment." Would that all public men had as nice an idea of the proprieties of politics! It is not the voice of the people that chooses the Governor of Zuñi, but the caciques.

The pueblo Indians have been repeatedly characterized as fire-worshippers. But with the Zuñis, at least according to Mr. Cushing, the principal object of their worship is water, just as was stated by Coronado. And well may they worship it, living as they do in the midst of a sun-parched land, their life dependent upon the life-reviving element so scantily bestowed! The writer will never forget how one day, as he was standing in the door of the Governor's house, the clear sky became overcast with black clouds. The Indians standing around cast anxious glances at the heavens; with the first drops of rain they all said, with an expression of unspeakable reverence gratitude, "E-la qua! e-la qua!" Which are their words for thanks.

A ZUÑI CHIEF.

One day there was a great excitement over a race between two fast ponies. A large crowd was collected, and betting was going on at a lively rate. All sorts of things were staked on the contest—cloth, skins, dresses, blankets, jewelry, harnesses, etc. These things were deposited in great heaps on the ground, and then, after all the bets had been arranged, everybody went down on to the plain to see the start. The riders were two lithe, light youths, entirely nude, and with long black tresses flying in the wind. It was a spirited, graceful sight as they dashed away at full gallop on their tough little steeds. They were soon out of sight in the distance. It was some time before they came to view again, for the course was a long one of about six miles. At last they appeared, two black dots, and coming nearer they were seen to be still neck and neck. The race was close, and there was but little distance between the two horses as they dashed past reeking with sweat. The crowd was intensely excited, and greeted the finish with a tumult of shrill yells. An old fellow, fat and good-natured-looking, who had taken an exceptional interest in the race, perhaps because of large stakes, cantered down to meet the contestants as they came in. But while away it seems that his mare threw him, for she came tearing back riderless and with saddle hanging loose, kicking it off as she neared the crowd. Some time after the old man came running back afoot, and as he came to a stop he said, emphatically, "Goddam!"—an expression which constitutes about all the English known in Zuñi. And as they do not know the meaning of that, its use can hardly be said to be sinful.

It was the day before the great dance. Everybody was getting ready for the holiday. All were to appear in their best clothing and with flowing hair, released from the little queues in which it is usually confined. Late in the afternoon we saw a young man sitting on a house-top with beaming face, while a brown beauty was carefully combing his hair as she stood behind. So the young man was a newly accepted lover! When a youthful Zuñi falls in love with a girl, he hints that it would be a real nice thing to have his hair combed. If she takes the hint and proceeds to comb it, it is a token that he has won her favor. The youth of Zuñi are just as sentimental, just as "spooney" in their love affairs, as fond of moonlight rambles and whispered nothings, as any lovers well can be.

As dusk deepened into night and the full moon rose over the roof-tops of Zuñi, there was a strangely beautiful sight. The narrow river meandered in a bright silver thread over the mysterious indefinite expanse of the plain. The stars glinted brightly in the intense blue of the marvelously clear sky, and looked down upon a new constellation. Fires gleamed on every house-top, lighting up great wall spaces with ruddy reflections, and sending tall shadows flitting round everywhere from the watching groups. The whole town was dotted with the fires, and it looked as if mild conflagration were in progress, feeding scantily upon such unpromising material as stone and adobe. These fires were kindled for the baking of the *hé-per-lo-ki,* or sacred festival bread, baked on the evening of every festival by the young maidens of the pueblo. Everywhere there was a contrast of strong light and deep shadow, the effect modified and softened by the floods of white moonlight. The groups of silent figures standing and sitting around formed compositions ready for an artist, and they were touched with Rembrandt lights.

Hé-per-lo-ki looks, and is said to taste, like Boston brown-bread. It is made by a rather peculiar process. The corn meal of which it is composed is chewed up by the young girls. The object of this is to sweeten it, for the acid of the saliva, uniting with the starch of thc corn, forms sugar. Some of the Zuñis, including the Governor's family, who can afford to buy sugar, make their hé-per-lo-ki in the way less economical, but more acceptable to civilized palates.

The morning of the festival dawned, and we were out early to see everything that was going on. All the town was in holiday dress. Everybody had his hair nicely combed, after washing it with amoli, the root of the yucca, or soap-plant, which makes the finest shampoo in the world, leaving the hair soft and glossy. The festivities were ushered in by the appearance of the "Mudheads," nude men painted a uniform mud-color from head to foot, and disguised with drolly hideous masks of the same hue, while several great knobs, like enormous wens, adorned a smooth head with a snouted countenance. The effect was irresitibly mirth-provoking; the characters looked like pantomine clowns just coming under the spell of Circe. The Mudheads ran through the streets, cutting queer antics, while they shot arrows into a bunch of feathers which they kept continually throwing on to the ground ahead of them. Then, after a while, the dancers made their first appearance, standing in a line in the street, and dancing and singing much as we had seen at Pescado. But now they were all arrayed in full costumes, and every performer was masked. After dancing solemnly for some time, they broke ranks and went back to the estufa, where the time was passed in their mystic solemnities until they appeared in another part of the town and continued their dance. Thus it went on through the morning, until the dancers had made the round of all the principal places of the town. At noon there appeared on the streets some frightful figures, hideous in the extreme and made diabolical in aspect by the buffalo horns which they wore on their heads. They ran along armed with great

THE HERALD.

bunches of reeds, and everybody scattered at their approach, for they were privileged to strike any person they met, and could inflict a blow not to be despised. There were shrieks of laughter as the crowds dispersed, running up ladders and scrambling over the house-tops. Whoever could get indoors was safe, for the horned creatures could not pursue them beyond a threshold. Courtesy toward the "men-from-where-the-sun-rises" would not have permitted them to molest us, had they overtaken us, but to please the people we joined in the fun, and pretended great fright, clambering ladders and fleeing until we were breathless. The spectators were convulsed with mirth at our apparent dismay.

The Zuñis have one annual dance expressly to frighten the children and keep them in good behavior the rest of the year. Characters even more horrible in appearance than those with the buffalo horns are the chief actors. They represent fearful goblins who come to devour and carry off the children. They make the round of all the houses in town, and at their approach the parents conceal their little ones, pretending to fight the demons off and defend their offspring desperately. This makes a lasting impression on the children, and the mention of these creatures has thenceforward the same quieting effect as our nursery bugbears, only the bugbears are made a reality to them. Formerly the Zuñis had a certain dance which took place once in thirty years. Its ceremonies required the sacrifice of a child. For the victim the worst child in the place was always selected. The mention of this festival was very apt to produce instantaneous good behavior in a contrary child.

The ceremonies of the morning were ended with disappearance of the horned monsters, and there was a recess of about two hours. At about three o'clock began the most imposing part of the exercises, which for the rest of the day were held in what is called Dance Place. This was a large rectangular court; on all sides the houses rose in terraces, forming a picturesque amphitheatre for such a solemnity. It was the most gorgeous natural spectacle we had ever seen in real life. Everything was so thoroughly in earnest about it; there was nothing that savored of the stage, nor was there evident any of the tawdry display customary to the parade days of civilization. It was a genuine manifestation of the deep religious feeling of the people. The costumes, which were generally highly grotesque, were splendidly elaborate, brilliantly beautiful in color, and rich in material. The genuineness of their make and the reality of the "properties" would put to shame the tinseled pretense of our gala days. There were wonderful varieties of headgear—plums, crests, beards, fantastic masks checkered off in various colors, evergreen decorations of spruce twigs arranged around the neck in a sort of a sylvan ruffle, or in a girdle around the waist; ingenious devices in the decoration of kilts, sashes, fine skins, while various kinds of antique-looking weapons, such as war-clubs, spears, and bows, ornamented with bunches of reeds, gave the scene a sort of heroically classical aspect. Many of the beards were of a pale Scandinavian blonde, while the hair was of the same color in a number of instances. Perhaps these might have represented mythological characters who were albinos. But the albinos had no beards. Is it not possible that they may point back to a time when a light haired and bearded race existed in America? The albinos of Zuñi—there were several in the place—were droll-looking figures; they looked like the Dutch peasants in the paintings of Teniers.

Thronging the terraced roofs of the Colosseum-like Dance Place were the spectators, their best apparel with its brilliant colors showing like a gay parterre, while on the upper line figures in brilliant hues, stood in intense sunlight against a deep, cloudless sky. All were gazing intently upon the dancers in the arena below, a line of stately rhythmic movement of rich colors, kaleidoscopic in its dazzling effect. From the dancers' throats arose a weird swelling song, accompanied by the jangling and rattling of rude instruments held in the hands and attached to the heels. This particular dance was called "the all-in-one," all the various dances of the Zuñi religion being represented in it.

CHIEF ON HORSEBACK.

Each figure impersonated some character in the Zuñi mythology. There were, for instance, the God of Water, the God of Fire, the God of Air, the God of the Cactus, the God of Turquoise, the Woman from the Moon, and the Echo God. A dance would last about ten minutes, during which the only motionless figures would be the Mudheads, who would stand around in groups, or sit upon the ground with a comical open-mouth air, and the priest of the dance, who was only unmasked participant. The priest was a handsome youth with flowing hair, dressed in a picturesque mediæval-looking costume of black buckskin, touched off with red sashes and abundance of silver buttons in rows. He wore knee-breeches and leggings, and looked as if he might have come out of the days of the troubadours. He stood statue-like at the head to avoid her as she endeavored to pluck the cactus adornments of his head-dress, and place them in the large basket she carried on her back. Meanwhile the Echo God, who was the last figure in the line of dancers, and kept invariably half a note and half a step behind the singing and dancing of the others throughout the whole, was at the end of the dance obliged to echo everything that was shouted out to him. He was thus often kept behind for several

BAKING HÉ-PER-LO-KI ON THE HOUSE-TOPS.

of the line of dancers, his position one of easy grace and he held a vessel of sacred meal in his hand. From this he would occasionally scatter a pinch of the meal on the ground. At a signal, which seemed something like that given in a theatre for a change of scene, the dancers would stop and retire for an interval of ceremonies in the estufa. As they were leaving the place, a bit of pantomine would always occur. The Woman from the Moon, who wore a skirt, and had a crescent-like mask, and long yellow hair streaming down her back—her whole aspect very Mother-Goose-like—would have a piece of by-play with the God of the Cactus, whose place in the line was just in front of her. The legend was that she had come down from the moon to gather cactus; therefore the God of the Cactus was trying minutes after the others had gone in. The mischievous Mudheads took a leading part in this diversion. We shouted out to him in English, and although ignorant of the language, he proved himself a remarkably clever imitator. But when one of us whistled, that was beyond his mimicry, and it seemed to disconcert him a little. Each of the impersonators had come into Zuñi in the early morning from the direction of the place where respective gods were supposed to live. The Echo God, for instance, came from his home in the valley near the sacred mountain.

The intervals between the dances were filled out by the antics of the Mudheads, whose functions corresponded exactly to those of the clown in a circus. Here was another of those inexplicable resemblances between Zuñi customs and those of our race. The Mudhead was an institution with them as far back as their traditions reached, and they had never seen anything in the nature of a circus. But, like our clowns, the Mudheads would burlesque the performance; they would get together and try to sing and dance like the regular performers, and would make the most awkward blunders, always resulting in failure and discomfiture. They would make a deal of clownish fun, showing that an acute sense of humor enters into Indian nature, the spectators greeting every sally with shouts of laughter as merry as ever resounded from the benches around a canvas-covered ring; and in their nude bodies, and heads smooth and bald, with exception of the knobby excrescences, they resembled the make-up of the traditional clown. As soon as the dancers appeared again, the Mudheads would subside, but would at once resume their indecorum with the beginning of the next pause. So it went on until the declining sun left the Dance Place in shadow. When its last ray had gone from the arena, the dance was ended. The handsome young priest approached the group of Mudheads, who stood with reverently bowed heads, and appeared to give them his benediction, sprinkling them with sacred meal. Performers and public then dispersed. That was our last day in Zuñi.